EYE ON KOREA

Joseph G. Dawson III, General Editor

Eye on Korea

AN INSIDER ACCOUNT OF KOREAN-AMERICAN RELATIONS

James V. Young

Edited and with an Introduction by William Stueck

TEXAS A&M UNIVERSITY PRESS • COLLEGE STATION

The paper used in this book meets the minimum requirements
of the American National Standard for Permanence
of Paper for Printed Library Materials, z39.48-1984.
Binding materials have been chosen for durability.

Library of Congress Cataloging-in-Publication Data

Young, James V., 1941–
    Eye on Korea : an insider account of Korean-American relations/
James V. Young ; edited and with an introduction by William Stueck.
        p. cm.—(Texas A&M University military history series ; 88)
    Includes index.
    ISBN 1-58544-262-3 (cloth : alk. paper)
    1. Korea (South)—History.   2. Korea (South)—Military relations—
United States.   3. United States—Military relations—Korea (South)
4. Young, James V., 1941–   I. Stueck, William Whitney, 1945–
II. Title.   III. Series.
    DS922.2.Y69   2003
    327.7305195'09'045—dc21   2002155082

CONTENTS

ILLUSTRATIONS

AUTHOR'S PREFACE

This story almost was never written. Following my retirement from the U.S. Army in 1990, I began a second career as an international business development consultant and had intended to work equally hard at improving my golf game. Business often took me back to Korea, however, and invariably into frequent contact with old friends in the army and U.S. State Department, and especially with my many Korean friends and associates from days gone by. Inevitably the talk would turn to our previous experiences in Korea, our affection for and interest in the country and the Korean people, and my own somewhat unique career and perspective as the U.S. Army's first fully trained and experienced Korea specialist. Friends often urged me to write a short review of my thirty years of experience in Korea, including the historic events in which I personally participated. After some thought and considerable procrastination, in 1994 I agreed to undertake this project for the Korean magazine *Wolgan Chosen.*

I wrote primarily out of a sense of history. Much had been written and published in Korea about such incidents as the assassination of Pres. Park Chung Hee in October, 1979, Chun Doo Hwan's seizure of control of the army the following December and the subsequent imposition of martial law, and the tragic events at Kwangju of May, 1980, but almost all of the published record was from the Korean perspective. In fact, when this memoir was published in Korea during 1994, there was no accurate account by any responsible American officer or individual who actually participated in these events.

Since then, Ambassador William H. Gleysteen Jr. and Gen. John A. Wickham have published in the United States their recollections of experiences in Korea during the late 1970s and early 1980s.[1] Yet these men served at the very top of the U.S. country team in Korea, and they did so over a short period of time. Neither was a Korea specialist. The recounting for an American audience of my lengthy experiences at the lower and middle levels—in Korea and in the United States—still seems useful for two reasons: first, my perspective on the events of 1979–80 are sometimes different than those of Gleysteen and Wickham; second, the transitional nature of the current

Korean-American relationship and the linkage of that process to events of the last two generations merits reflection and comment by one who was involved over the long haul.

With the assistance of William Stueck, a historian at the University of Georgia, I have adapted my story into this English-language edition. The adaptation has involved some additions to and subtractions from the original as well as some reordering of materials and some updating of analysis to take into account events of the last several years. Professor Stueck also has added an editor's introduction and citations to place my narrative in the context of what others have written and the archival documentation now available. Yet the basic story remains the same. Because this is a recent history, many of the participants are still living. Some have been contacted and interviewed for this book, but most have not. It is based primarily on my own memory—I did not keep a diary or take more than rudimentary notes, for it was previously never my intention to write of my experiences. Also, unless the individuals have given specific permission or are so well known as to be "public" people, I have not used their names in order to protect their identity. This is particularly appropriate when discussing the activities of certain Koreans who were cooperating and providing information on the activities of the Korean military during the period between the assassination of President Park and the rise to power of Chun Doo Hwan. Often these brave and patriotic individuals were cooperating at risk to their careers and personal safety, and their efforts to help Americans understand the true situation as it developed were invaluable. Few are still on active duty in the Korean military; most are engaged in business activities or living quiet lives in retirement. Regardless of their present circumstances, they are deserving of privacy.

Historians are ever on the lookout for new sources. Most of them come in the form of written documents from the period of events described and are tucked away in government archives, private libraries, or even people's attics. For the historian of the recent past, the sources are sometimes oral or, if written, exist in the form of memoirs covering the experiences of an individual going years, even decades, into the past.

In the case of the document presented between these covers, I was fortunate enough to meet the author in 1995 at the annual conference on Korea sponsored by the Richard L. Walker Institute for International Studies at the University of South Carolina. I was beginning research for a history of U.S.-Korean relations and was particularly interested in the American role in South Korea's democratization. Colonel Young, I discovered, had been stationed in Seoul in 1979–80 and again in 1987, both key periods in the Republic of Korea's circuitous path toward an open political system. I came to look forward to our yearly meetings, where I could pick his brain both for knowledge and wisdom about America's relationship with Korea.

Eventually I discovered that Young had published an account of his experiences in serialized form in a Korean magazine. Although encouraged by Ambassador Walker and others to adapt his story for an American audience, Young procrastinated, uncertain that he wanted to put the time and effort into the project. It became my goal to bring that procrastination to an end. Finally in May, 2000, while once more enjoying Ambassador Walker's hospitality and listening to Young reminisce about his Korean experiences, I worked up the courage to ask him if I could assist in preparing for publication an English-language edition. He agreed and provided a manuscript for my examination.

The manuscript did not disappoint. Written in a direct, unpretentious style, it offered frequent displays of the sharp wit and intellect that I had come to enjoy in him through personal contact. It also told the fascinating story of Young's Korean odyssey, from his first assignment on the peninsula as a junior officer in the early 1960s through his retirement from the U.S. Army in 1990 and his trip a year later to North Korea as a member of an unofficial delegation of prominent Americans. Here was a tale from which Americans could learn a good deal about their relationship with Korea over a thirty-year period.

Of particular interest was the fresh, firsthand account of the controversial events of 1979–80 leading to Chun Doo Hwan's takeover of the South Korean government. As the assistant military attaché in the U.S. Embassy, Young did not always agree with the cautious approach taken by Ambassador Gleysteen in the aftermath of Pres. Park Chung Hee's assassination in October, 1979. Young's narrative represented the first by an insider to outline alternatives that were widely discussed at the time. Equally important, he examined the major personalities involved—their strengths, their limitations, and their perspectives—in a manner that added new insights into why the United States behaved as it did. What emerged was an account that added important new knowledge and perspective to one of the most tragic episodes in the history of U.S. relations with Korea.

The material covering Korean events of 1979–80 was far from the only contribution of the manuscript. There were also fresh accounts of the infamous tree-cutting incident of 1976, the controversy over Pres. Jimmy Carter's plan in 1977 to withdraw U.S. troops from Korea, the successful move of the Republic of Korea toward democracy in 1987, the Seoul Olympics of 1988, Ambassador Donald Gregg's efforts to combat anti-Americanism in South Korea during 1989–90, and a 1991 initiative by Gen. Richard Stilwell (U.S. Army, retired) to explore an opening to North Korea. In all these cases, Young showed a keen appreciation of the importance of personalities, bureaucratic politics, and country expertise (or the absence thereof) in influencing outcomes.

Despite the manuscript's obvious merits, it was clearly written for a general Korean audience. People and places well known to most Koreans were often mentioned without explanation; conversely, personalities and institutions on the U.S. side were sometimes described in a manner that would seem patronizing to Americans. In addition, the manuscript had been produced largely from Young's memory, rather than from personal papers and other written documents. To enhance credibility before an American audience composed largely of scholars and other observers with a particular interest in Korea, the information presented needed to be checked as much as possible against other available sources. Finally, there were sometimes gaps in the story that required exploration to ensure that no significant memory from Young's rich experience failed to come to light.

Over the past two years, it has been my pleasure to work with the author in eliminating these problems. Basic information on Korea has sometimes been added to the text, while unnecessary data on the U.S. side has been cut. Extensive research has been done in the presidential libraries of Gerald R. Ford and Jimmy Carter and in scholarly and journalistic sources involving U.S.-Korean relations. In a few cases this has led to corrections in details in the original text. More often it has resulted in the addition of citations either to document points or to refer readers to sources that elaborate upon them. Finally, I have asked Colonel Young to search his memory to provide elaboration on some points. At his own initiative, he has added chapters on his 1996 experience negotiating a business deal with North Koreans and reflecting on his four decades of engagement with Korea. The result, I believe, is a story that remains largely the same as before but will prove more crisp, more clear, occasionally more detailed, and overall more credible to a broad audience of Americans interested in Korea.

Far too often our understanding of important events is compromised by the failure of participants after the fact to invest the time necessary to record their memories. Those who do take the time are usually people at or near the top of governments or private institutions. While the resulting stories represent valuable historical documents, they are written from particular perspectives and often leave out critical information. With this in mind, we should be especially grateful to Young, for he provides careful accounts of many pivotal events in the Korean-American relationship from the perspective of a lower- or middle-level official who nonetheless possessed expertise beyond that of most of the people he served. However we judge his conclusions, we cannot ignore the information and the insight he provides.

William Stueck

EYE ON KOREA

CHAPTER 1

Preparation

I was born just prior to World War II at, appropriately for one who would become a military officer, an army airbase in Michigan. My mother, Alta Duncan, was the product of a pioneering family of Scot, Irish, and Cherokee heritage, with roots in the Deep South. My father, Ernest Young, was originally from northern Indiana, but then his father took an engineering professorship at Oklahoma A&M (now Oklahoma State) University in Stillwater, where my parents met and married. By 1942 my father was serving overseas and had become a highly decorated fighter pilot in what was then the U.S. Army Air Corps. He was killed in 1944, while we were living at an air base in Oregon. After his death we moved back to Oklahoma. My mother held a college degree and placed a high value on education, so we eventually settled in Oklahoma City, where she felt my younger brother and I would receive a good education in the public schools. Mother remarried in 1948 to a young lawyer, G. M. Fuller, who later became one of Oklahoma City's most prominent citizens. He was my Dad from that time on, a special person and role model, and our family life was generally harmonious.

I was a little wild in high school, having a weakness for pretty girls, motorcycles, fast cars, hunting and fishing (sometimes pursued while classes were in session), and an occasional 3.2 beer, the only alcoholic beverage legally available in Oklahoma at the time. Yet I managed to make the varsity wrestling team and to perform rather well in English, Latin (those being the days when public schools really provided an education), and history. I went on to attend the University of Oklahoma, graduating in 1963 with a major in political science and minors in English and history.

Originally set on becoming a lawyer, I soon discovered that I was not fond of law school and left after a year and a half. While an undergraduate, I had taken four years of ROTC, the first two because they were required at all land-grant colleges, the last two because of the urging of my parents and the thirty-dollar monthly salary, a decent sum in those days. At the time, nearly all young men had to serve in the military, and the choice was between be-

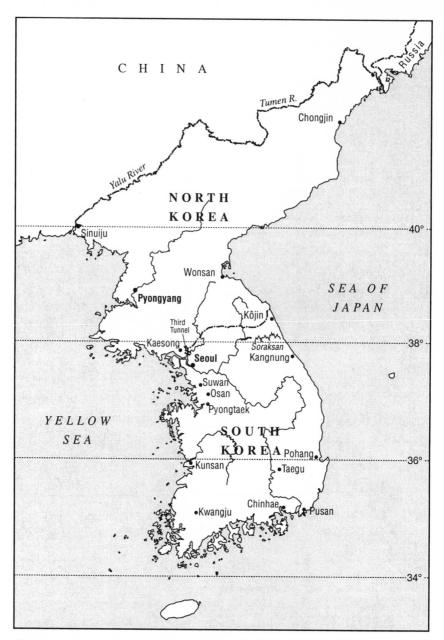

Map 1. Korea, with place names mentioned in the text. The broken line at the thirty-eighth parallel is the armistice line agreed upon at the end of the Korean War. **Map drawn by Wendy Giminski, Campus Graphics and Photography Department, University of Georgia.**

ing drafted and entering as a private or taking ROTC and entering as an officer. The latter sounded better to me. Although I never intended to make a career of the army, it turned out that I enjoyed military life.

Like most Americans, I had little interest in or appreciation for Asia as a boy and only remember seeing the newspaper reports concerning the Korean War, which was the first time most of us had heard of such a place as Korea. After the war ended in 1953, Korea retreated to the far reaches of my memory.

This rapidly changed in the early and middle 1960s. I married Jody Elston, my high school sweetheart, in 1960, and after graduating from college and leaving law school, I was commissioned a second lieutenant in the U.S. Army. When officers' basic training was completed, I received orders to Korea for my first duty assignment.

I reported at the end of 1963, remaining until early in 1965. This first assignment in Korea, which unknown to me at the time would be the first of several, was a great learning experience. Korea was far more rural then than it is today—and poor, very poor. Every U.S. unit supported a school or orphanage. The kids were usually in bad shape by our standards and did not seem to get much government support. We provided things like clothes, a small amount of financial support, some food and milk—whatever we could. Some of my soldiers who had carpentry or other skills would also sometimes help with building projects and repairs on weekends. For a young, middle-class American, the whole country, except for parts of Seoul, was pretty much the pits. The only paved roads I remember were but a few miles long—from Seoul northwestward to Kimpo Airport and from Seoul southward to Suwon. The air terminal at Kimpo was little more than a Quonset hut; the military arrivals entered one side and civilians (of which there were few) entered the other.

I was initially assigned to a unit in the Osan/Pyongtaek area, which was just south of Seoul and not far from where, in July, 1950, American troops had first engaged (disastrously) the North Koreans in battle. Soon, however, I was selected to take charge of another unit that was located well in the rear, in North Cholla Province near the town of Kunsan. This unit had its troops deployed at about a dozen different sites over a large area, and I became quite familiar with the Cholla geography and people. In the southwestern part of South Korea (officially the Republic of Korea, or ROK), the Cholla Provinces were even more depressed than most of the rest of the country—poor sanitation, subsistence farming on small plots, and little opportunity. It was only later that I became fully aware of the regional animosity that existed between the Cholla people and other Koreans, especially those from the Kyongsang Provinces to the east.

Living conditions for a young officer in Korea during the early 1960s were adequate but far from comfortable. I lived in a small Quonset hut, which also housed my three senior noncommissioned officers. There was a centralized space heater that was designed to radiate heat throughout the hut but seldom did this very well. Shower and mess facilities were shared among myself (the only officer), the NCOs, and the enlisted men. My duties required me to travel most of the time to check on my widely dispersed troops. Life on the road in those days was a real adventure due to the poor road conditions and bridges that were susceptible to seasonal flooding and other problems. Nonetheless, I managed to visit my soldiers and check on their operational status, living conditions, and concerns on a regular basis.

Monthly paydays were particularly eventful. It took almost a week to reach all my soldiers. Troops were paid in Military Payment Certificates, printed by the armed forces, rather than greenbacks, this being before the days of direct deposit and computerized accounting. The payroll officer was always armed, for there were reported to be occasional bandits who would steal the payroll, although I never encountered any such problems. Pay in those days was very low—my own salary was less than $250 a month, and my soldiers received considerably less. Yet I sent most of my money home and even saved a considerable percentage since there was little to spend it on. (Today when I read about grossly inflated corporate salaries and Hollywood alimony payments of six figures per month, I do not have a lot of sympathy.)

Recreational opportunities were few. We had an older-model movie projector and watched a movie about twice a week; we also received a monthly box of paperbacks from the USO. The U.S. airbase at Kunsan, which was about a two-hour drive from my platoon headquarters, had a gym, small library, bowling alley, and club facilities, where one could get an occasional "restaurant-type" meal. Other than that, we were pretty much left to our own devices for diversion. Several of my soldiers enjoyed hunting, and some of us would hunt pheasants and ducks in the fall and winter. We had two or three mixed-breed camp dogs that, with a little training and experience, turned into good bird dogs. My favorite was named Pabo, which is the Korean word for "crazy," and she was a devoted hunter and companion. Regrettably, a few weeks after my return to the States, I learned that Pabo had fallen into the hands of some local residents and had been eaten, a not uncommon fate for dogs in those days (even today dog meat is consumed by some Koreans). At any rate, by Christmas Day, 1964, we had accumulated enough pheasants and ducks that we invited over one hundred local Koreans onto the compound for a Christmas dinner. Among the guests was Raymond Burr, a TV actor famous for his portrayal of Perry Mason, the criminal lawyer. Mr. Burr made a habit of visiting troops overseas each Christmas, and his appearance at our small outpost was a real treat for my soldiers.

Over the course of that initial assignment, it became apparent to me that most American soldiers, even the officers, were poorly prepared for duty in Korea. Not only were we unable to speak the language but we were also totally ignorant concerning Korean customs, history, and culture. I made many clumsy mistakes in dealing with ordinary Koreans that I look back at now in embarrassment—for example, entering a house with my boots on, being too direct in addressing issues with Koreans, and such. I vowed that if I ever returned to that country, I would be better prepared.

In early 1965 I was reassigned to the United States, where I spent about eighteen months assigned to an air-defense unit near Kansas City and later attended the Armor Officers Advanced Course at Fort Knox, Kentucky. Following this was a transfer to Hawaii for a staff assignment with the Pacific Army Headquarters. By this time the Vietnam War was going strong, and I was ordered to join the 1st Infantry Division in Vietnam in late 1968. I served with the 1st Division for several months and saw combat often. I was wounded, though not badly, and recovered quickly enough to be given command of a company in the central part of Vietnam north of Qui Nhon. My company's area of operations included a territory we shared with both South Vietnamese troops and a Korean division, though with few American units in the area other than my own.

My experience with the South Vietnamese forces was not always positive. Our company was a small and somewhat isolated unit, and in the event we were attacked by a larger enemy force, we were dependent upon the nearby friendly forces to assist us with artillery fire and ground reinforcements. In more than one case, the Vietnamese failed to respond, and once they even mistakenly fired their artillery directly into our positions, wounding several of my men and narrowly missing me. Frustrated by this, I contacted my battalion headquarters, explained the situation, and requested that either American or Korean units be reassigned as my backup unit, replacing the South Vietnamese. After several days with no response, I decided to take matters into my own hands and directly contacted the commander of an adjacent Korean unit.

The difference between the Koreans and the South Vietnamese was like night and day. The Korean commander immediately agreed to give us all possible support within his authority. By nightfall the same day, he had sent a subordinate officer to work out the details, and I went to sleep that night for the first time with a feeling of confidence. Our relationship continued to improve throughout my time there. On the day I left, the Korean commander presented me with a bottle of *InSam Ju* (wine with a Korean Ginseng root in the bottle) as a departure present. As I wished this fine officer a fond farewell, I sensed the loss of a good friend and reliable ally, a feeling that was to grow as I had more experience with Koreans in the years to come.

Upon returning to the United States, I faced an important decision. I had been in the army for seven years. Along with many of my comrades, I had become disillusioned by the Vietnam War. Most of us were in our middle to late twenties, old enough and smart enough to have private doubts about our government's involvement there, yet we had been determined to do our duty as officers and soldiers. We felt we had achieved that goal while enduring the frustrations caused by severe restrictions on our operations, working with a less than ideal indigenous ally, and the lack of public support for the war. We also believed that we deserved better upon our return than the mixed reception we received from our government and the American people. I almost decided to leave the army and return to civilian life, but at the last minute changed my mind.

Earlier I had heard of an experimental army program in which certain officers with skills in politics, language aptitude, and other diplomatic-type skills could enter a special training program. This was designed to train selected officers for duty that required close and continuous contact with foreign countries and their military. Usually such officers were assigned to high-level staff duty or to embassy duty, advising senior officers or civilian officials on policy concerning their respective countries. After some thought, I decided to apply for the program and to stay in the army if accepted. Each applicant was allowed to select three countries, in order of preference. I thought carefully about which countries were the most interesting and provided the most possibility for an army officer to have a satisfying and rewarding career. I then wrote as my three choices, in order, Korea, China, and Japan. I was soon notified that I was awarded my first choice and eagerly began to prepare for training as a Korea specialist. Later I learned that I had been the first officer selected for the Korean Foreign Area Specialist (FAS) Program.

If my first assignment in Korea had made me wish for better preparation prior to assignment, the rigorous training of the FAS program satisfied all those desires in full. The program was intense, difficult, and demanding. Only about one-third of the applicants were selected, and not all of those selected actually completed the program, which included a year of intense Korean-language training, a year at a civilian university for an advanced degree, and a year of specialized orientation and travel in one's selected area. My first stop, after picking up my wife, Jody, and two young sons, who had been waiting for me in Hawaii, was the Defense Language School in Monterey, California. I found the Korean-language course to be the most difficult phase of the training, and finished only in the middle of my class despite working very hard. In fact, learning Korean is a nightmare for most Americans—the structure is backward from English, the grammar convoluted, and the words are hard to pronounce and very alien to us. The level of speech is dictated by the relationship between the two parties in terms of status, age, position, and other factors. The same thing can be said several different ways, even using different words, depending on the relationship of the speakers. Korean has one of the highest dropout rates at the Defense Language School, and even the graduates seldom achieve real fluency in the language. In later years, those of us who did manage to graduate decided that the reason Korea maintained its independence for so many centuries while surrounded by powerful neighbors was that no one on the outside could ever understand the language.

Following language training, I attended the University of South Carolina for a year, obtaining a master's degree in international studies, with East Asia as my major field. My professor and mentor that year was Richard L. "Dixie" Walker, who at the time was teaching East Asian politics and heading the International Studies Department. Professor Walker was a big influence on me, and I developed much respect not only for his wide knowledge of Asia but also for his courage as an administrator. For example, because of widespread opposition to the Vietnam War, army officers were not welcome on most college campuses in those days. Professor Walker not only accepted me and several other officers as students but also actively recruited us and made numerous special efforts to make us feel welcome. This resulted in a special bond between us that has continued to this day. In later years, the University of South Carolina continued to attract army officers to its Asian studies program, and there became a significant number of alumni and classmates who studied under Professor Walker. Soon he was jokingly referred to as the "Godfather of the Korean Mafia," especially after Pres. Ronald Reagan nominated him to be ambassador to Korea in 1981. But this jumps ahead of my story.

After graduate studies, the army sent its FAS officers to an in-country training phase for one or two years, depending on the country in which they specialized. For some countries, such as the Soviet Union, there was a well-established training program already in place. These officers were sent to Garmish, West Germany, where they further developed their area expertise by traveling in Eastern Europe and parts of Russia and improved their language skills. Since I was the first specialist on Korea, no such program was in effect for that country. In 1972 I was assigned to the U.S. Embassy in Seoul and the Defense Attaché Office for the purpose of training and also developing a program of instruction for those Korea specialists who would follow. This was to be the first of three assignments to the embassy.

The defense attaché at the time was Col. Donald Hiebert, who had served in Korea previously and had been a liaison officer with the Korean forces in Vietnam. Colonel Hiebert had a long career in the army's Special Forces and as a result knew most of the Korean Army's Special Forces officers quite well. One of his frequent associates was a young colonel, Chun Doo Hwan. Hiebert had met the colonel in Vietnam, where Chun had commanded a battalion, and had continued their association in Korea. They met rather frequently. I recall meeting Chun for the first time at the U.S. ambassador's residence during the summer of 1972 and once or twice after that, usually accompanied by Colonel Hiebert. Hiebert was also acquainted with several others from the Korean Military Academy Class 11, such as Roh Tae Woo and Chung Ho Young, but I believe he was best acquainted with Chun.

Chun had the earmarks of a comer. He was part of a close-knit group, all from the Taegu area, who had been in the first class to graduate from the academy with four full years of education. That class had been selected to attend the academy from a talented pool of applicants, literally the cream of the crop of high school graduates during the Korean War. Chun himself was of average height, somewhat stocky, and carried himself with a bit of a swagger. He was very direct for a Korean, efficient, intelligent, and bold—capable of making decisions without a lot of hand-wringing analysis. He already possessed a rather impressive following in the army and had been selected for early promotion several times. He spoke adequate English and had little difficulty communicating with Americans.

In addition to becoming acquainted with present and future leaders of the Korean military, the goals of the training program were to improve language skills, learn the Korean military system, and assimilate as much Korean culture, history, geography, and economics as possible. I accomplished much of this by study as well as by traveling extensively within the country.

In 1972 South Korea was much more developed than it had been when I left seven years before. Major highways were paved; there was a superhighway from Seoul to Pusan, and another from the east coast to Seoul was almost completed. There were far more automobiles. People had higher expectations and were more confident in their abilities and future prospects. Yet travel was still a little difficult in some areas, and I was determined to see all of the ROK and become familiar with each of its regions.

Over the next year I traveled more than thirty thousand kilometers throughout South Korea. I used every possible means of transportation, including car, train, bus, military and civilian aircraft, and even an occasional turnip truck. (I would sometimes hitch a ride on a small truck carrying turnips or cabbage to help me get to know Koreans better; one does not learn much or improve one's language capability driving around in an embassy sedan.) Later I purchased a small motorcycle and drove it to every province of the ROK, taking five weeks to do so. My ten-year-old son accompanied me on part of that journey, clinging closely to my waist with wide eyes all the way. (Today he is a grown man and business executive, the father of four children of his own, but we still fondly remember that adventure together.)

In the late summer and early fall of 1972, I walked from Kojin near the Demilitarized Zone (DMZ), the border with North Korea, to Pohang, a journey of six weeks that also consumed two pairs of hiking boots. The modern highway along the eastern coast had not yet been completed, so much of this journey was along unimproved roads or footpaths. I explored the rugged beaches and fishing villages of the scenic east coast and made side trips to such areas as Kyongpodae, a lake near Kangnung where Korean royalty used to vacation during the hot and humid Korean summer, and Soraksan, the spectacular park of jagged peaks and abruptly rising mountains often referred to as the "Rockies of Korea." At Soraksan I climbed Bisundae Mountain, slept under the stars, shared a meal with several Buddhist monks, and drank from the mountain streams. In the city of Kangnung, I stayed for two or three days while waiting for a resupply of hiking boots and money from my office. I was warmly treated there by the proprietor of a small *yogwan*, who provided accommodations despite the fact that I was temporarily out of money and must have looked like a tramp, having just come from the mountain experience at Soraksan.

I encountered many other acts of kindness from ordinary Koreans during this trip, and it was a highlight of my second tour in the country. Seoul is an exciting and vibrant city, but I think the real heart and soul of Korea is in the countryside.

By the time my in-country training was complete, I knew the landscape better than most Koreans and had friends and acquaintances in almost every part of South Korea, even the smallest towns and villages. This experience made a big impression on the way I thought of the Korean people. During my travels, I had been befriended in countless ways, taken into homes for a meal, and offered shelter. Koreans had a reputation for being cool to strangers, especially foreigners, but this was not true to my experience, then or later. I had developed a deep affection for the people.

On a less positive note, I began to recognize the pervasive influence and invasion of privacy that Koreans in those days were forced to accept as a normal part of life. In October, 1972, President Park imposed martial law nationwide, and a month later he pushed through the authoritarian "Yushin Constitution," which among other things set the stage for his continued rule on an indefinite basis. A series of national and international developments—a narrow reelection victory for the president in 1971, the withdrawal of a division of American troops from the ROK while the United States rapidly scaled down its effort in Vietnam, U.S. overtures to the Communist regime in China, and the opening of talks between North and South Korea—created intense insecurity among the top leaders of the South Korean government. Park's response was to tighten control over his surroundings, a development that affected Americans in South Korea as well as that nation's citizens.[1] Government security officials always seemed to know where I was going and what I was doing. Since I was assigned to the U.S. Embassy, I had been warned that the security apparatus would be watching my activities, and indeed there almost always seemed to be someone who would appear each day to ask me where I was going, the purpose of my visit, how long I was staying, and such. Some of this was perhaps natural curiosity, but too often a black jeep would appear out of nowhere to watch my movements. For all the time the authorities spent watching me, they must have been disappointed when my activities always amounted to nothing more than attempts to improve my poor language capability and learn more about the local area.

Near the end of my assignment during the summer of 1973, I was asked to write a report summarizing my year at the embassy so that those who followed would not have to "relearn" the lessons I had already learned. The report was fairly extensive and recommended that future officer trainees attend the ROK Army Staff College at Chinhae as part of their training. It also recommended that, due to the difficulty of the Korean language, future trainees spend at least two years undergoing formal language training. Both of these recommendations were approved and implemented, and to the best of my knowledge, they are still part of the Korean Foreign Area Specialist Program today. The final section of the report dealt with my impressions of the ROK armed forces, particularly their army. At this time I had neither the expertise nor the background to write a truly comprehensive or detailed report, but I did make some points that would later prove to be quite prophetic. These points are paraphrased as follows:

My experience with South Korean forces in Vietnam and my observations over the past year have convinced me that the ROK Army is a first-class fighting force. They are well disciplined, physically tough, and adapt well to training. The individual Korean soldier is in every way equal to or in some cases superior to his American counterpart. Their officers are generally competent and intelligent. They plan cautiously, and for every conceivable contingency, prior to deployment. They are generally by-the-book in regard to their tactics. Weak points may be a certain lack of flexibility and a system that does not always reward innovative thinking. At the higher levels their generals sometime appear more concerned with politics than with strictly military matters.

Generals in the United States are hardly novice in the ways of politics, but their South Korean counterparts during the 1970s and 1980s were in another league—a reality that I had only begun to comprehend.

CHAPTER 2

Into the Fray

I n early 1973 I was assigned to the Office of the Assistant Chief of Staff for Intelligence, Headquarters, U.S. Army, at the Pentagon in Washington, D.C. After almost four years of training as a Korea specialist, I was now ready to become a contributor to the policy process, though admittedly at a low level. I entered this assignment during a time of stress in U.S.-Korean relations. The American withdrawal of a combat division from the peninsula in 1971, the rapid reduction of American forces in Vietnam, the acceptance at the beginning of 1973 of a disadvantageous armistice there, and the improvement of U.S. relations with the People's Republic of China created deep anxieties and uncertainties in the ROK government.

Most military officers dislike Pentagon duty, and I was at first no exception. I was placed in charge of the Northeast Asia Desk, which included North and South Korea and Japan. Basically my responsibilities were to be knowledgeable concerning all military, political, and other developments that could have an effect on the region, particularly from the army perspective. Each morning I prepared briefing materials and input for the army chief of intelligence, Maj. Gen. Harold Aaron, on any significant events in my area. This was then incorporated into another briefing, which was given to the army chief of staff as appropriate.

My experience in Washington gave me an appreciation for American intelligence gathering that I could not have developed otherwise. Information was available from the Central Intelligence Agency (CIA), the Defense Intelligence Agency (DIA), State Department, and other sources that could be analyzed rapidly. Often desk officers and analysts in Washington or in other major headquarters knew more about a situation than the commanders and ambassadors in the field, for they had a lot more information available and more means with which to analyze it. I formed the opinion then that you could probably find enough reporting information to reach almost any conclusion, including one that totally contradicted another. There was simply an enormous amount of reporting coming in—often too much. Each morning there was a large stack of intelligence reports just in my Northeast Asia area alone—at least several inches of paper every day. Later, when some individuals claimed they had had no prior warning about such events as occurred in Korea in 1979–80, I had to believe that the warning signs had been there in intelligence reports all the time, if someone had been doing proper analysis. But such scrutiny was not easy, given the volume and diversity of evidence available.

The First Korean Nuclear Crisis

One of the issues I dealt with was nuclear weapons. The problem concerning North Korea's atomic capabilities and intentions, which has received headlines since about 1990 (and in 1994 nearly led to war), is not the first nuclear controversy on the Korean peninsula. During the mid-1970s, the issue of nuclear weapons development forced a serious confrontation between the ROK and U.S. governments and brought Korean-American relations to a crisis point.[1] As an army intelligence officer in the Pentagon, I had a unique vantage point from which to watch this drama unfold.

In the 1960s the South Korean Army depended on the United States for almost its very existence, including its weapons, organizational and tactical doctrine, logistics, and even most of its basic wartime supplies, such as ammunition. The Korean government realized that this was not in the long-term interests of the nation and was determined to improve the ability to independently produce its own defense material, ammunition, and weapons. As a result, during the late 1960s Korea embarked on an ambitious program to become self-sufficient in the domestic production of defense equipment.

By the early 1970s the United States and the ROK were working together to improve Korea's defense capabilities. Much of the emphasis for this effort came directly from Pres. Park Chung Hee. Indeed, to my way of thinking, most of the credit for Korea's strong military today can be traced back to initiatives begun under the Park government. I think that he was probably the most farsighted of all the modern Korean leaders in this respect.

The U.S. government initially supported the domestic production of such items as small-arms ammunition and rifles. U.S. companies such as Colt and others provided technology in order to assist the development of these industries. This policy cooperation has generally continued through the present day. In fact, what began as a fairly modest defense industry under President Park has now expanded to the point where South Korea produces most of its own defense equipment, including ships, aircraft, missiles, and other sophisticated and technologically advanced weapons. Occasionally Korea and the United States have had different opinions about the development of certain weapons systems or the transfer of technology, but these differences have usually been worked out to the mutual satisfaction of both sides.

In the early 1970s, however, Park began a secret program to develop an entirely different type of weapon, a move that was understandable given uncertainties created by the U.S. effort to scale down its responsibilities in Asia. Yet his action brought cooperation between the United States and South Korea to a decisive crossroads.

Nuclear proliferation had not been of major concern to the United States before the early 1970s. Conventional wisdom at the time was that it would be very difficult for most nonnuclear countries to successfully develop and produce an atomic weapon without substantial outside assistance. The U.S. intelligence community was confident it could detect any attempts made to obtain such assistance. But this assessment proved to be incorrect when, on May 18, 1974, India tested a nuclear bomb. The Indian explosion caught all Western intelligence agencies by surprise. Neither the CIA nor DIA, which was somewhat of a fledgling organization at the time, had predicted this event. Even the British intelligence service, which had better information about India than the Americans, failed to correctly understand the Indians' intentions. At any rate, this event caused a major reexamination of our nuclear proliferation policy.

The U.S. intelligence community was ordered to make a full-scale investigation into the capabilities and possible intentions of other countries that might be tempted to follow the same path as India. As was the customary procedure, the CIA took the lead in this project, with assistance and support from the DIA, the military-service intelligence organizations, and others. A few weeks later, a "Special National Intelligence Estimate" (SNIE) on the subject of nuclear proliferation was published within the government. For the U.S. intelligence community, publication of a SNIE is a particularly important event. SNIEs are normally produced only at the direction of the White House or the director of central intelligence on subjects of immediate and critical interest to the president. Accordingly, a large amount of resources are devoted to the topic.

This SNIE was an analysis of several countries that we believed had the capability to produce a nuclear weapon if the political order were given. Israel was of primary interest, and it was the opinion of the SNIE that the Israelis probably had already developed a nuclear weapon. As for South

Korea, the estimate of the American intelligence community in 1974 was that it would need perhaps another ten years to develop such a weapon without outside assistance.

The SNIE was intended only as a point of departure for more detailed analysis of several other countries considered to have a possible interest in manufacturing nuclear weapons, including Pakistan, Brazil, and Iran. Pakistan was thought most likely to pursue such a policy and was high on the watch list. Near the end of 1974, however, we were studying information on a number of other countries, including the ROK, because nonproliferation had become such a major concern of the U.S. government.

In an effort to determine if any of those countries might be attempting to develop a nuclear weapon, we analyzed a number of different factors. One was the existing threat to each nation. In this area South Korea ranked high because of North Korea and its strong military capability. Another consideration was human resources, that is, whether or not the country had the scientific and technical expertise to produce a weapon. In this area Korea again ranked high due to its intelligent and well-educated professional class and good scientific and engineering capability. A third factor was the ability to manufacture a weapon from domestically available industrial materials and equipment. Korea ranked low here. We estimated that the Koreans would have to import a significant amount of material and equipment, such as power reactors, uranium fuel, and other items. The fourth factor was political will. At the time, there was no firm evidence that the ROK had this, a situation we expected to continue as long as the U.S. security guarantee was in place. This later proved to be an inaccurate assumption.

As part of our efforts to determine whether Korea might be moving toward a nuclear weapons capability, we began to systematically review what information we already had available. Beginning with a detailed and extensive list of components and equipment that could be used in a nuclear weapons program, we examined import-export licenses and requests and began to pay much more attention to reports from other countries. It soon became evident that the ROK was actively investigating the international market for a number of items on the list and had actually purchased some of them. Also, Korea was negotiating with the French for a fuel-reprocessing facility capable of extracting plutonium and with another country for the purchase of a nuclear-fuel laboratory capable of further processing plutonium.[2]

About this time we also became aware of field-intelligence reports indicating that we might have misjudged the intent of President Park to continue to rely solely on the American nuclear deterrent. Of special interest were reports of a certain high-level weapons-development committee that recommended the development of new weapons systems to the Blue House (the ROK equivalent of the U.S. White House). According to one such report, this committee had informed President Park that development of a nuclear device was feasible and had recommended that Korea go forward with it. With these reports and the clear evidence that the ROK was attempting to purchase many of the necessary components from a wide variety of international sources, the U.S. intelligence community in early 1975 determined that Korea was most likely attempting to develop nuclear weapons.

Following this determination, a series of meetings occurred in Washington to decide how to deal with the problem. Along with Japan, our closest Asian ally, South Korea had many supporters, particularly in the Defense Department. On the issue of nuclear proliferation, however, there was almost total agreement that development of a Korean nuclear weapon would be destabilizing and would probably lead to attempts by other countries in the region to build their own weapons. There was particular concern that, if South Korea was successful in this program, the Soviet Union would assist North Korea in building a nuclear weapon or that Japan would rethink its existing nonnuclear policy.

In an unusual unanimous agreement, U.S. policymakers decided to take all necessary measures to convince the South Koreans to abandon this project. The next step was to determine how we could pressure them to do so.

At the time, the United States had been assisting South Korea in developing its peaceful nuclear power program. The American company Westinghouse Corporation had already supplied two small research reactors, and Korea had expected to build several civilian nuclear power plants over the following years. These plants were past the design stage; in fact, one was already under construction. There were also ongoing plans and programs to train a substantial number of Korean nuclear technicians in the United States. Further, the ROK's peaceful nuclear power program was to be financed in large part by low-interest loans and U.S.-guaranteed loans. Some of this money was from the U.S. Export-Import Bank directly and was to be used for equipment, construction, reactors, and fuel purchases. It was clear that we had fairly substantial technical and economic leverage vis-à-vis the civilian nuclear power program that could be used if necessary.

The United States also had obvious leverage related to defense. South Korea was under the protection of the U.S. nuclear umbrella. It also enjoyed the guarantees of the mutual-security treaty with the United States, backed up by the visible presence of American forces forward-deployed on the

Korean peninsula. There was little support for threatening to withdraw our forces or suspending the mutual-security treaty, but it was always possible if other methods failed. Withdrawal of the U.S. nuclear umbrella, however, was considered to be a legitimate alternative, especially if Korea persisted in developing its own nuclear capability.

After analysis of our options, authorities decided that a diplomatic initiative would be formed to present an alternative to President Park. This would be done directly and forthrightly. The strategy would be to convince him that he had more to gain by abandoning his nuclear weapons plan than he had by continuing it. For example, if Park was agreeable to give up his bomb, the United States would agree to continue to work in a positive manner to assist Korea's peaceful nuclear power development. This would not only include the Westinghouse plants already under construction but future plants as well. Also, the United States would continue to provide loans and other financial incentives for the continued construction and development of these facilities and expand technical training opportunities for Koreans studying nuclear engineering and similar subjects in the States.

If, given these alternatives, President Park insisted on continuing with his nuclear weapons project, stronger action would be taken. This might include such measures as mentioned earlier up to and including strong threats to limit the future U.S. commitment to Korea's defense. In this regard even Korea's strong supporters in the Defense Department were prepared to consider and implement such options.

The fact that Korea was working on a nuclear weapon was, of course, quite sensitive information, limited to certain members of the intelligence community and a close circle of top policymakers in the U.S. government. Because of the close relationship between South Korea and the United States, special precautions were taken to make sure the media did not become aware of the situation. Our greatest fear was that there would be a news leak before we could mount a diplomatic approach to the Blue House.

The key players in the diplomatic initiative were Ambassador to Korea Richard Sneider and Assistant Secretary of State Philip Habib. Of the two, Habib was the more influential and played the most important role. As a former ambassador to Korea himself, Habib knew President Park well and had his confidence. He also had substantial credibility with the Blue House and a reputation for a no-nonsense approach to diplomacy. Some diplomats have a tendency to disguise their message in protocol or indirect language, but this was not the case with Habib. The U.S. government knew it could count on him to deliver its message in a straightforward and frank manner.

Sometime in the spring of 1975, the American delegation began to broach the issue of Korea's nuclear plans with the Blue House. The initial discussions were not particularly helpful—the Koreans were reluctant to admit the existence of such a program. Indeed, many top-level officials were not even aware of the program because of its great secrecy. Most of these initial contacts were conducted personally by Ambassador Sneider, and the reports of their outcome were forwarded to Washington through a special private channel. The tone of these reports was somewhat discouraging. Sneider was particularly unhappy that the Koreans were not forthcoming enough to admit the extent of the nuclear program. He believed that we would eventually have to reveal the extent of our actual knowledge from outside intelligence sources. I recall that Ambassador Sneider at one time said, "At some point we will simply have to tell the Koreans 'NO.'" I interpreted this rather abrupt statement to mean that the United States was prepared to use maximum leverage in order to stop the nuclear program.

By the summer of 1975, President Park had been convinced to abandon nuclear weapons development. My understanding was that Assistant Secretary Habib played the critical role in persuading Park. Both men are now dead, and only they know the full story, but I believe that Habib actually threatened several actions. Among these was a total withdrawal of American support for Korea's nuclear power program, including technical information, training, and all existing loans and loan guarantees in support of plant development. Further, Habib threatened a "complete review" of U.S.-Korean security arrangements, including our nuclear umbrella. But if President Park agreed to cease his nuclear weapons program, these existing programs would not only continue but also be enhanced and expanded.

In June, 1975, President Park stated to the news media that South Korea would be forced to develop its own nuclear weapons capability if the United States withdrew its nuclear shield.[3] This statement caused a great outcry and brought requests for clarification from several quarters. Some people interpreted this statement to be a veiled threat designed to force the United States to continue its security guarantee to Korea—"or else." In truth, I believe that President Park was only stating in an indirect way the obvious alternative solution to this problem—that as long as U.S. nuclear protection *did* extend to Korea, he would abandon his plans to build atomic weapons.

The evidence from June, 1975, forward strongly supports this conclusion. By the fall of 1975, our intelligence reports indicated that South Korea was no longer investigating the world market for nuclear-related equipment, and we had received private assurances that the Korean nuclear program was indeed terminated. In early 1976 Korea withdrew from negotiations with the French for the nuclear plant that would have been capable of reprocessing plutonium. That same year U.S. grants and loans for Korea's peaceful nuclear power program were expanded and work on the existing and planned Westinghouse plants accelerated. By 1978 Korea's first major nuclear power plant was in full operation. The ROK-U.S. security alliance, which had been tested by these events, had survived intact.

Some may say that the American "hardball" tactics employed during this period were unfair and bullying. That may be a reasonable criticism, but this was an issue of great importance, one that we clearly felt strongly about. In the final analysis, we were successful in preventing the development of a South Korean bomb because we had good political, economic, and security ties and, therefore, were able to use the applicable leverage in those areas to our advantage. The ultimate result was probably the best outcome for both countries.

The Panmunjom Tree-Cutting Incident: How a Second Korean War Almost Began

The Demilitarized Zone in Korea has always been a dangerous place. There have been serious incidents between the military forces of both sides on numerous occasions, and some of these have led to deaths. In August, 1976, one of the worst of these events took place—the axe murders, or tree-cutting, incident.[4]

The ROK and the United States maintain a small force at Panmunjom. These soldiers are specially selected and are assigned to a combined unit of approximately company strength. Their mission is to protect U.S. interests in the Joint Security Area (JSA), where the Military Armistice Commission meets. The North Koreans have a similar force, and each side has the right to maintain guard posts, perform routine maintenance, and generally move freely about the area in the performance of its duties.

As part of these normal duties, on August 18 a small detachment from the ROK-U.S. side was engaged in trimming a large poplar tree that had become overgrown and was blocking the vision between two of the U.S. guard posts. As they worked, a group of North Koreans approached them, at first only observing the activity. Soon the mood turned ugly. The North Korean officer in charge suddenly ordered his men, who were armed with axes, metal pipes, and other weapons, to attack. Two American officers were singled out for special attention during the attack and were brutally murdered with axes.

When this incident was reported to U.S. Forces Korea (USFK), there was some initial confusion. Gen. Richard L. Stilwell, then the USFK commander, was in Japan at the time and immediately made arrangements to return to Korea. By the time he returned, planning had already begun in Seoul and in Washington for an appropriate response to the North Korean atrocity.

Because of this crisis and my background as a Korean specialist, I was recalled from my normal duties and assigned temporarily to the intelligence section of the emergency-action team for Korea, located in the Pentagon's National Military Intelligence Center (NMIC). My job was to monitor North Korean forces, with which I was familiar because of my recent experience on the North Korean desk in the Army Intelligence Office.

After the initial meetings to determine how to respond, there were several options to consider. One was to lodge a stern protest through the Military Armistice Commission but to avoid any military retaliation. The second option was to launch a limited military operation into North Korea. This would not be a full-scale invasion force, but one that would have limited objectives. It would nonetheless be a forceful, punitive raid designed to inflict casualties and provide a lesson to the North Koreans that they could not get away with murder without serious and substantial retaliation. The first option was rejected as too weak, the second as too strong. Eventually it was decided that the best response would be one that had limited objectives, did not run the chance of leading to all-out war, would still intimidate the North Koreans, and get the message through that we were not playing games. Both the USFK and the South Koreans began planning such an operation, with support and assistance from the Joint Chiefs of Staff (JCS) in Washington.

As finally approved, the plan had four elements. First, military forces in Korea would be raised to a higher defense posture, Defense Condition 3 (DEFCON 3). The purpose of this move was precautionary to some extent, but our real hope was that by increasing our own readiness condition, the North Koreans would move into defensive positions. By doing so they would be less able to launch an attack. A few hours after we began moving our forces and conducting the other activities associated with DEFCON 3, the North Koreans took the bait. Their forces moved into their prepared defensive positions, where they would need more time to mobilize and regroup if they intended to take an offensive posture.

The second element was to greatly increase our intelligence coverage of the North. Especially important for this was the role of our SR-71 high-altitude spy planes. We flew numerous missions near the DMZ, which both gathered important intelligence information and caused the North Koreans to activate their target-tracking radars at their missile units. This provided us with perfect location data, which was relayed to our artillery and missile batteries. Had the North Koreans decided to actually launch a missile, we would have been able to destroy the launch site within moments.

The third element involved a massive mobilization of U.S. air power, which was somewhat controversial. It called for launching F-111 and B-52 strategic bombers, which would aim their direction of approach straight at Pyongyang. These were nuclear-capable weapons platforms of which the North Koreans were aware, although they could not know whether or not they actually carried nuclear weapons. We also had large numbers of carrier-based naval aircraft launched and were careful to make sure that all these aircraft gained sufficient altitude to show up on North Korean radar screens.

The fourth and final element of the plan was ground action at Panmunjom. This part of the plan would involve a ground force of approximately eight hundred men with the mission of entering the Panmunjom area rapidly and with surprise, cutting down the tree that had caused the original confrontation, and destroying two illegal gates that had been constructed by the North Koreans. It was hoped that the small force of about sixty men actually involved in the tree-cutting operation would be able to go in, complete its mission, and withdraw without making contact or provoking an incident with the North Koreans.

The actual entry force comprised two platoons, one American and one Korean, and a small engineer contingent with chain saws, which would actually cut down and remove the tree. Since the armistice agreement forbade the use of heavy weapons inside the JSA, these men were armed only with sidearms and ax handles. Backing them up, however, was a significantly more capable force, including two artillery battalions, one Korean and one American, that were instructed to fire on order at prearranged targets. These batteries actually had ammunition loaded in their artillery tubes and were prepared to fire immediately. Also deployed on the ground just outside the JSA was a South Korean infantry company. A U.S. infantry company was in position aboard helicopters just south of the DMZ. Other armed helicopters and fighter aircraft were assigned to orbit the area in support of the ground forces. The entire operation was codenamed Operation Paul Bunyan.

Most of the detailed planning for this operation took place in Seoul, but it could not proceed without approval from Washington.[5] As we reviewed the operational plans during our approval process, our intelligence team also double checked the targets that were preapproved for artillery bombardment and airstrikes should these become necessary. One of the immediate targets was a North Korean army barracks near the DMZ where most of the North Korean Army's reinforcements for the Panmunjom area were billeted. During this process, we noticed in the same general area as these barracks one target that seemed to be a small cottage. On closer inspection I could identify this as the quarters of the Czech-Polish delegation, members of the so-called Neutral Nations Supervisory Commission. Somehow this structure had made its way onto the target list. The error was immediately reported to the operations section, and the cottage was removed from the target list. With this important modification, the overall plan was approved for execution.

Yet soon, difficulty arose between the JCS and USFK over command-and-control issues. The JCS desired a direct communications link with the task force commander, Maj. Gen. Morris Brady, who led the 2d Infantry Division. General Stilwell was determined to resist such contact because he did not want to run the risk of his field commanders getting direction from Washington without those orders going through him. To ensure that Washington would not be countermanding his orders, Stilwell instructed his staff to refuse any attempt by the JCS or the White House to establish direct communications with any of his subordinate units. This eventually resulted in a rather heated argument between the JCS and USFK senior staffs, but General Stilwell held firm.

There was also an attempt by the U.S. Embassy in Seoul to become directly involved. Ambassador Sneider had just returned to Korea from the United States a few hours before the actual operation was scheduled to begin. He took a chair in the bunker at Yongsan next to Stilwell, who was on the telephone giving last-minute instructions to General Brady. Sneider attempted to take the telephone from Stilwell's hand and speak directly to Brady. Stilwell held on to the telephone firmly, refusing to let go. Sneider pulled, Stilwell pulled back. Finally Stilwell won. "Was there something you wanted to ask General Brady?" asked Stilwell. Sneider gruffly replied, "Well, I am the president's personal representative in this operation." Stilwell smiled at Sneider and replied, "Of course, I will be happy to relay any questions from the president to *my* field commanders."[6]

Despite these competitions between the Pentagon and USFK and the embassy and USFK, when the operation actually began, it was conducted with skill and success. My experience has been that soldiers on the ground can almost always be counted on to perform well as long as they are given good training, adequate resources, and strong leadership. That was again true in this case. The combined ROK-U.S. task force entered the JSA at 7:00 A.M. and by 7:45 A.M. was finished with its business. The tree was no more, and there had been no resistance or violence from the North Koreans. The story should have ended there, except for an incident involving General Brady's helicopter, which almost caused a disaster.

By virtue of being the 2d Division Commander, General Brady was also the Paul Bunyan ground commander. In Vietnam it had not been uncommon for helicopter pilots to fly low over the jungle in order to draw fire from enemy forces. While this tactic had some value in Vietnam's heavy jungles, in the open terrain of Korea, it was both foolish and dangerous. Around ten o'clock in the morning, long after the actual tree cutting had been completed and the ground task force withdrawn, Brady ordered his command-and-control helicopter to fly along the JSA close to the North Korean positions. The North Koreans responded with automatic-weapons fire, hitting the aircraft, which fortunately was able to return safely. This incident came dangerously close to triggering our contingency plans for activating our artillery fire and other counterattack forces. Later, USFK stated officially that Brady's helicopter had been on the southern side of the JSA and blamed the North Koreans for the incident, but several eyewitnesses to the event believe his helicopter was very close to or even over the line, and the North Koreans might have had a legitimate right to fire at it.[7]

Most Korean and American citizens only learned about this operation after it was completed. They were told that it had been a great success. It was successful, but squabbling between various elements over command and control and Brady's helicopter incident were omitted from or distorted in official reports. We had an excellent plan that was well executed, but except for some good luck, we could have had a serious military confrontation on our hands.

Although my primary interest was in the military situation, particularly regarding North Korean military forces and capabilities, I also was expected to be knowledgeable concerning events that could cause instability in the ROK. The U.S. government had several overriding interests in Korea, but the primary concern was security. The major threat to security was North Korea, but the State Department was also concerned that human rights conditions in the ROK under President Park would eventually result in internal problems and instability. After nearly losing a presidential election to Kim Dae Jung in 1971, Park had imposed the authoritarian Yushin Constitution and created what was close to a police state. The prevailing view in Washington was that this was a mistake but that as long as the U.S.-Korea security alliance held firm, South Korea would be secure from external attack. U.S. policymakers also believed that Park had done a good job with the economy, and a continuing strong economic picture would blunt criticism internally for his lack of democracy. Human rights was not important enough to "rock the boat" and risk instability.

This all changed with the election to the presidency of Jimmy Carter in 1976.

James Young as a U.S. Army second lieutenant in early 1964 at his unit's base camp during his first assignment to Korea.

Young in early 1969 in South Vietnam following a patrol outside the Lai Khe base camp with the 1st Infantry Division.

American and South
Vietnamese officers
in late 1969 in the
Cha Rang Valley.
The officer in the
center (and to the
author's right) is
Col. Lee Kak Li, who
escaped after the
Communist victory
in 1975 and became
maitre d' at a fine
restaurant in
Minneapolis.

Young's official
photograph as
assistant defense
and army attaché at
the U.S. Embassy in
South Korea,
September, 1977.

U.S. presidential motorcade in Seoul, June, 1979.

President Jimmy Carter stands to Pres. Park Chung Hee's right in a Seoul ceremony. Park's daughter, Park Keun Hye, stands to Carter's right, and First Lady Rosalyn Carter stands to Park's left.

A South Korean soldier keeping watch across the Demilitarized Zone during the summer of 1979.

*General John Wickham (extreme left) and Ambassador William Gleysteen
(extreme right) confer with visiting U.S. officials Thomas B. Ross, assistant
secretary of defense for public affairs (second from left), and Adm. Maurice
Weisner (second from right) just weeks before Pres. Park Chung Hee's
assassination.*

*Colonel Ahiro Hagino, the
Japanese military attaché in
Seoul during the events of 1979–
80, with Young in 1980.*

ROK soldiers and tank at a university campus in Seoul during the first day of full martial law in May, 1980.

Paul Wolfowitz (left), then assistant secretary of state, and Richard Armitage (right), then assistant secretary of defense, with Young and his wife in the Pentagon, 1985.

Ambassador Richard L. "Dixie" Walker with Young at the ambassador's residence in Seoul around August, 1985.

Major General Kim Jin Young and James Young near Taegu in the fall of 1987.

Kim Jin Young and James Young enjoy a moment of camaraderie in the attaché's residence at the Yongsan U.S. Army compound. Later, when Roh Tae Woo became president, Kim became a lieutenant general, the capitol security commander, and eventually the chief of staff of the ROK Army.

Young with Korean officers at a formal function, a common duty for military attachés.

Ambassador James Lilley (center), Young, and members of the South Korean National Assembly aboard the aircraft carrier USS Kitty Hawk in 1988.

Ambassador James Lilley with South Korean National Assembly members on the deck of the USS Kitty Hawk. James Young is on the extreme left.

The famous Third North Korean Tunnel, discovered in October, 1978.

Young with ROK Minister of Defense Lee Sang Hoon, his wife, and the U.S. Air Force crew chief of the aircraft that carried the group during a tour of the United States in 1989.

Lieutenant General Yong Young Il, the director of the ROK Defense Intelligence Agency, shares an informal meal with James Young during the spring of 1990.

Colonel Young at his retirement and award ceremony in the U.S. Embassy, July, 1990, with his wife and Ambassador Donald Gregg.

In the Hall of Deputies (the North Korean National Assembly), Pyongyang, 1991.

Young enjoying retirement in Virginia in 1994, with a Korean chest and other memorabilia. The photograph on the chest was taken with General Richard Stilwell in Pyongyang in 1991.

CHAPTER 3

The Rise of the Troop-Withdrawal Issue

Although the success of Operation Paul Bunyan demonstrated the ability of the ROK and the United States to work together in a military context, the mid-1970s was often a period of suspicion between the two countries, especially on the diplomatic front. Much of this distrust can be traced to decisions made in Washington, with minimal consultations with Seoul, yet having a direct effect on South Korea. The Nixon administration's unilateral withdrawal of one infantry division from the peninsula in 1971 is a prominent example. Unfortunately the Carter administration's policy toward Korea would be even worse.

Jimmy Carter ran for president at a time when the American public and many in Congress searched for alternatives to the traditional Cold War direction of U.S. foreign policy.[1] After over a generation of presidential domination in that area, the legislative branch reasserted itself. In addition to cutting funds for support of the anticommunist regime in South Vietnam, thus expediting its fall in April, 1975, congressional reformers launched an in-depth study of U.S. covert operations abroad and pushed for the adoption of human rights criteria as a prerequisite for continued support to allied governments. This development led to increasing criticism of the ROK, and as a presidential candidate Carter sometimes joined in the attack. He even proposed, over time, the removal of American ground troops from the peninsula.[2]

Nonetheless, even after Carter was elected in November, 1976, neither I nor most of the people with whom I worked were greatly concerned about relations with the ROK. We were fairly confident that once he was sworn in as president and had access to more information, such as the secret intelligence estimates of North Korean forces, he would not actually follow through with his strict human rights policy. American politicians, as politicians in all democracies, have a habit of making many promises during a political campaign that are impossible to keep after being elected. But this case turned out to be different, and the result was a deterioration in U.S.-Korean relations that would span the entire four years of the Carter presidency.

The Struggle Begins

President Carter began his term of office with some bad advice about the Korean situation. Some of his advisers in the area were inexperienced and had a built-in bias not just toward South Korea but all countries with a military government. They tended to be extremely critical of the Park government's record on human rights but virtually ignored human rights conditions in other countries, including North Korea. This attitude unfortunately tended to blind them to the realities of the Korean peninsula, especially the importance of maintaining a strong U.S.-ROK security alliance. The Carter team did not appear to take the North Korean military threat as seriously as the Nixon and Ford administrations had, believing that, with its strong and growing economy and well-trained military forces, the ROK could provide most of the muscle for its own defense. Among those who may have been influential were Jerome Cohen, a peace activist who played an important role in drafting a portion of Carter's campaign platform relating to Asia, and retired Rear Adm. Gene LaRocque, who was a strong advocate for the withdrawal of American ground forces from Korea.

Only a week after Carter's inauguration on January 20, 1977, the White House forwarded to the Joint Chiefs of Staff the top-secret Presidential Review Memorandum 13 (PRM-13).[3] This document asked for a military opinion regarding which of three options was preferable for the withdrawal of American ground forces from Korea. It is significant that PRM-13 did not ask for an opinion from the JCS as to the military effect of such a withdrawal, only which option was preferable. The three alternatives differed only in timing—one was immediate withdrawal, one was withdrawal over a two-year period, and one was withdrawal over a four-year period. None was acceptable to the JCS, which they reported to Secretary of Defense Harold Brown. After some additional consultation with the Joint Chiefs, however, Brown informed the White House that the four-year option was the preferable of the three.

The White House directed that U.S. Forces Korea was not to be consulted on this matter. To not confer with the field commander on such an important issue as this was almost unheard of. Speculation at the time was that the Carter administration was trying to avoid alerting the South Korean government that PRM-13 was being considered. Also, Gen. John W. Vessey Jr., the USFK commander, was certain to be opposed to the withdrawal and would fight it vigorously, so from the administration's viewpoint, perhaps the less he knew the better. In this Carter and his supporters were correct, but it was naive of them to think they could keep such a secret from either USFK or the Koreans for very long.

A few weeks after PRM-13 was circulated, I had dinner with General Vessey and several other officers at the residence of the commanding general of the army's Combined Arms Center at Fort Leavenworth, Kansas. General Vessey had just returned from Washington, where he had briefed President Carter on several issues, the focus being on the new intelligence estimates of North Korean strength. Vessey also presented several other well-reasoned arguments that U.S. ground forces should not be withdrawn from the peninsula. He expanded on these reasons during our dinner, observing as well that he believed President Carter had not been properly briefed by his staff and was now rethinking his previous decision. At this point, I believe, General Vessey thought that the troop withdrawal issue was going to be reexamined and probably overturned. Unfortunately he was mistaken.

The New Intelligence Estimate

Reassessment of the military strength of potential enemies is a common occurrence, and such a process involving North Korea had begun shortly after President Ford's visit to the ROK in November, 1974. That event was part of a longer trip to the western Pacific, which included meetings with Japanese and Soviet leaders in Tokyo and Vladivostok respectively, and was aimed at highlighting the ongoing U.S. commitment to South Korea's defense. ROK officials expressed concern about a military buildup by North Korea, about the same time we began a study of its forces.[4] The extended review process came to final fruition just before Carter entered office, and the product could not have been more clear-cut in its conclusions.

After an initial army study had revealed larger concentrations of enemy armor and artillery near the thirty-eighth parallel than previously estimated, Maj. Gen. Harold Aaron, the army's intelligence chief, decided sometime in late 1975 or early 1976 to conduct a complete top-to-bottom review of North Korea's force structure. Long a believer in Korea's importance to the United States, both strategically and politically, my boss wanted the review to use all available information sources, including satellite technology. As the army's Korea desk officer, I was responsible for overall staff supervision and coordination for this top-secret project, and we began to identify intelligence specialists who were familiar with North Korean forces from previous assignments and background. Eventually over forty such individuals were identified worldwide and brought to Washington, sometimes at considerable expense, to conduct the study.

The senior member of the study team was John Armstrong, a bright, young West Point graduate, now a civilian, and he and his team worked night and day, seven days a week, on the project. At the finish we had accumulated a huge amount of information on North Korean forces and had literally counted every tank, armored personnel carrier, and artillery piece in their inventory. The results were astonishing—not only was the North Korean Army significantly larger than the U.S. and ROK intelligence community had previously estimated but also its equipment inventory and deployment pattern indicated conclusively that it was an offensive-oriented force capable of attacking the South with little or no warning. The findings were initially challenged by the U.S. Defense Intelligence Agency and the CIA, but in every case our army analysts were able to conclusively defend their findings, methodology, and conclusions.

The Washington bureaucracy churns out dozens of such intelligence reports every year, but few of them have any lasting influence. This one was different, partly because it was completed just before Carter entered the White House and began pushing for troop withdrawals and also because General Aaron had for months moved energetically behind the scenes to ensure that it received widespread attention. I remember writing numerous back-channel messages for him to senior officers in South Korea, the Pacific area, allied counterpart organizations, and senior officials in Washington to communicate the results and orchestrate reactions. Thus, when the final report emerged, it was not simply another in a large pile, but rather a widely anticipated challenge to conventional wisdom.

When in March, 1977, General Vessey reviewed the findings with Carter, the president seemed impressed. It was during my dinner with the general at Fort Leavenworth shortly thereafter that he stated his belief that the commander in chief would seek further consultations with him before reaching a final decision on troop withdrawal.[5]

The Struggle Escalates

When Army Chief of Staff Bernard Rogers visited Korea late in April, however, there was no indication that troop withdrawal would be reconsidered. In fact, at a private U.S.-only luncheon at Ambassador Sneider's residence, General Rogers stated that it was the common opinion in Washington that

Carter intended to follow through on his earlier plan to remove ground forces from South Korea.[6]

Following Rogers's departure from Korea, there was a meeting at the USFK Yongsan headquarters to determine the next step. General Vessey was adamantly opposed to the withdrawal but was obligated to carry out the president's wishes if he were so directed. Until he received such orders, however, he was determined to do everything possible to convince the administration to change its policy direction.[7]

A number of people in both Seoul and Washington agreed with Vessey. An informal plan gradually took shape in opposition to troop withdrawal. The first component was the education of the press. Active-duty military officers, of course, have to be extremely careful about what they say to the media, something Maj. Gen. John Singlaub, General Vessey's chief of staff, would soon demonstrate. Former officers, however, have considerably more freedom. General Stilwell, who was recently retired, had excellent access to the press in Washington and other influential media, such as *Foreign Affairs* magazine, the *New York Times,* and *Newsweek,* among others. With strong support from other retired and active officers, he began a writing campaign in many of these important publications. He also began to lobby members of Congress and organize opposition to the Carter plan in various veterans' organizations and other groups. This effort was effective in getting our message to a large and influential segment of the American public.

Another component of the opposition plan was to educate and alert Congress to the dangers. It was particularly important to persuade congressmen to hold hearings on the troop-withdrawal plan before the Carter White House was able to make it a *fait accompli.* Despite the efforts of General Stilwell and others, though, we had been only partially successful in generating support in Congress until the early summer of 1977, when we received unexpected assistance from a very surprising source—the *Washington Post.*

The *Washington Post* was an unlikely ally in opposing the Carter plan because it had consistently supported the president and his policies and was generally thought to agree with his position on Korea. The *Post* had been critical of ROK president Park for many years, particularly of his human rights record. In May, 1977, in Seoul, *Post* reporter John Saar interviewed General Singlaub on the overall topic of troop withdrawal. Singlaub, whom I saw often in later years, maintained that he was treated unfairly during the now-famous *Washington Post* interview that resulted in his removal from his position at USFK.[8] The general did not dispute the accuracy of what was reported, only that he considered his remarks to be on background and, therefore, not for attribution or direct quotation. Regardless, in the interview he was quite critical of President Carter's policy, and these remarks became the centerpiece of a front-page story in the *Post* within twenty-four hours. At midnight of the same day that the story ran, General Singlaub was directed to report to the White House immediately.

Upon his return to Washington, Singlaub found that he could expect no support from the senior leadership of either the army or the Defense Department. In meetings in the Pentagon before reporting to the White House, General Rogers accused him of being an embarrassment to the army, and Defense Secretary Harold Brown gave him neither support nor encouragement. Singlaub's subsequent encounter with President Carter went no better. The general was given no real opportunity to defend himself and was simply told by Carter that he had "lost confidence in his [Singlaub's] ability to carry out his instructions." According to General Singlaub, the entire meeting lasted only a few minutes, with Carter displaying his trademark ear-to-ear smile the entire time.[9]

For those of us who hoped to overturn the Carter withdrawal plan, the Singlaub incident was a blessing in disguise. Until then we had had considerable difficulty getting adequate publicity for our side of the case. Our most valuable tool was the new intelligence estimate of North Korean forces, but this information was classified and could not be openly released to the news media. Singlaub's dismissal, however, was big news. Carter and his staff had now ensured that the Korean troop-withdrawal issue would be debated with a new intensity. Indeed, within hours after the *Washington Post* article appeared, Congressman Sam Stratton of the House Armed Services Committee requested that General Singlaub be permitted to testify before his committee on the issue. This request was approved, and Singlaub appeared before the committee only two days after his meeting with Carter.

Congressional committee hearings are of two types, open and closed.[10] The open sessions are for unclassified testimony and are open to the media; closed sessions are more informal and can include classified information not available to the public. During closed sessions in this case, General Singlaub outlined in detail the new estimates of North Korean forces, describing them as forward deployed and fully prepared for war with little or no warning. He also briefed the committee on the results of a recently conducted USFK wargame that indicated that, even with the U.S. 2d Division in place, our combined ROK-U.S. defense capabilities were not capable of adequately defending the city of Seoul with any degree of confidence. This shocked the congressional committee. At the end of the long day, which included more than seven hours of testimony, Congressman Stratton, the chairman, announced that he would directly challenge the Carter troop-withdrawal plan.

Within days, columnists and editorial writers across America began to question the wisdom of Carter's policy.[11] The existence of our new intelligence estimates began to leak out, and additional members of Congress joined Stratton in criticizing the Carter plan. Congress was also concerned that it had not been officially advised or consulted or had an opportunity to debate or discuss the withdrawal plan. Interestingly these events occurred as Gen. George S. Brown, chairman of the Joint Chiefs, and Philip Habib, undersecretary of state for political affairs, consulted President Park on the withdrawal issue in Seoul. They returned to submit a top-secret report emphasizing the need to assuage Korean concerns for "compensatory actions" in the form of large-scale transfers of U.S. military equipment. Such transfers would require congressional approval.[12] In stirring up a hornet's nest on Capitol Hill, the Singlaub affair was the best thing that could have happened for those of us opposed to troop reductions.

In fact, things were going so well after the Singlaub incident that it was widely believed within Korean circles that Generals Singlaub and Vessey actually conspired to set this scenario in motion. One story even said that they had flipped a coin to determine who would sacrifice their career in order to help defeat the Carter policy. Both men denied this story, but I do strongly believe that the battle to overturn troop withdrawal would not have been fought so ferociously had the administration been more honest and open with the military about its plans. In this case, they were simply devious and untruthful about their real intentions.

For example, Carter and his staff, particularly Secretary of Defense Brown, on several occasions indicated to the media and others that the JCS, who were the president's senior military advisers, had agreed with and supported his policy. This was a misstatement. When PRM-13 was circulated, it had only offered the three withdrawal options and had pointedly not asked for an opinion as to the wisdom of the policy itself. Despite this the JCS had volunteered their opposition. Brown, however, had reported to the White House that the more lengthy withdrawal option had been the choice of the JCS. Carter also had stated his intention to consult with General Vessey before making a final decision on the matter; he failed to do so. It was only much later, and even then only after Congress forced policymakers to reexamine the new intelligence data on North Korean forces, that Vessey's views received a full hearing.

The final action that galvanized the military opposition to the Carter withdrawal plan was the failure to be forthcoming and upfront on this matter, either to the Korean government or to those who were charged with the responsibility to carry out U.S. policies in Korea. Specifically, both USFK and the U.S. Embassy in Seoul were officially informed in May, 1977, that no final decision had been reached on the troop reductions and that the Habib-Brown visit to Korea in late May would be for the purpose of discussing and negotiating this issue with our Korean allies. In reality, President Carter had already made the decision, having signed a decision memorandum to that effect early in May, *before* the message announcing the visit of Habib and Brown and without any prior consultation with the Korean government. In this way the Carter White House had not only misled the Korean government but also the senior American leadership in both USFK and the embassy. I believe that this duplicity was one reason such dedicated officers as Generals Stilwell, Vessey, and Singlaub, in addition to others who were working actively behind the scenes, were willing to forcefully confront the White House.

Retaliation

Perhaps embarrassed by the public success of thwarting the withdrawal plan, the Carter administration made several attempts to punish those who had worked against it. General Singlaub was forced to retire a few months after his removal as USFK chief of staff. General Stilwell suddenly found his Pentagon privileges restricted and was denied the type of access and respect normally afforded a former four-star officer and major commander. General Vessey was suspected of being involved in sabotaging the troop-withdrawal plan and was "punished" in a very unusual way.

Following his assignment to Korea, General Vessey's name was put forth to be chief of staff of the U.S. Army. Although the president formally nominates the officer for this position, in all but the most unusual cases, he accepts the recommendation of the army's senior leadership. In this case Vessey was the army's overwhelming choice. Carter, however, had different plans. When Vessey's name reached his desk, Carter abruptly summoned him to Washington for a personal interview. The general, who was still in Korea at the time, flew for sixteen hours directly to Washington and reported immediately to the White House. At the "interview" Carter asked Vessey what he thought about his troop-withdrawal plan, which by this time was dying a slow but certain death. The general replied truthfully, stating that he believed the plan was a mistake and hoped it would not become policy. Carter then asked him what his original goals had been when he entered the army. Vessey, who had entered the army during World War II at the rank of private, replied that his original goal had been to become a First Sergeant. The president then indicated that the interview was over; it had lasted about five minutes. Vessey, having no further business in Washington, returned to his airplane and flew the sixteen hours back to Korea.[13]

Carter subsequently chose Edward Meyer, one of Vessey's former subordinates and a three-star officer, to be chief of staff. He then offered the job as vice chief of staff to Vessey, probably with the expectation that the general would retire. Instead, Vessey accepted the position and served with great distinction as the army's number-two man. After Carter was defeated in the next election, Ronald Reagan elevated General Vessey to chairman of the Joint Chiefs of Staff, the highest position a military officer can hold. He also appointed General Stilwell deputy undersecretary of defense for international security policy. General Singlaub became an unofficial adviser and consultant to the Reagan administration on a number of issues.

The Civilian Side

Not all the opposition to Carter's withdrawal policy was confined to the U.S. military. There were several key members of the president's own staff who, once in place and better educated as to the true Korean situation, also voiced opposition. Their disagreement was less obvious and open than that of men such as Stilwell and Singlaub, but it was at least equally effective.

The major civilian players in this drama were Assistant Secretary of State for East Asia and Pacific Affairs Richard Holbrooke, Assistant Secretary of Defense for International Security Affairs Morton Abramowitz, and National Security Council Staffer Michael Armacost. All three were Carter political appointees. Of the three, Holbrooke, a fierce bureaucratic infighter who chaired the Interagency Group on East Asia, was the most active in quietly working to reverse the policy.[14]

Intra-administration opposition to troop reductions was not based directly on the Korean situation or concern over North Korea's military strength. Instead, it was based on regional political considerations. Holbrooke and others believed that withdrawal from Korea would send signals of U.S. weakness in Asia at precisely the time when we should be displaying strength. American strategic interests in the Asia-Pacific region were increasing. The relationship with China was rapidly developing, and other Asian countries were looking to the United States to show its resolve to remain a Pacific power following the collapse of South Vietnam. This was, in their view, the worst possible time to withdraw any forces from Korea.

The civilian strategy was to declare support for Carter's plan officially and publicly while delaying its actual implementation. Rather than directly challenge Carter as Generals Stilwell, Singlaub, and to some extent Vessey were doing, Holbrooke cleverly arranged to delay certain orders and action memoranda that would have pushed the withdrawal schedule forward. By bureaucratic maneuverings of this sort, he allowed time for Congress to become further involved in the process, for public opposition to grow, and for the intelligence community to expand on and refine the detailed army study of North Korean forces that would eventually result in the policy's defeat. Holbrooke and his supporters were working quietly and were quite concerned following the Singlaub affair. They believed that such overt actions as pursued by Stilwell and Singlaub would only cause Carter to further harden his attitude toward Korea, and they probably viewed the generals' actions as unsophisticated.[15]

An important problem for Holbrooke was that two key players in the Carter administration, National Security Adviser Zbigniew Brzezinski and Undersecretary of State for Political Affairs Philip Habib, supported the president in his withdrawal policy. As a former ambassador in Seoul who was considered the ultimate Washington expert on Korea, Habib was a critical supporter. Despite his background, he held a somewhat negative view of the need for U.S. ground troops in the ROK.[16] Above all, he was extremely loyal to Secretary of State Cyrus Vance, who in the early stages also supported Carter's plan.

The "delay and further study" tactic employed by Holbrooke and his supporters obviously could not continue indefinitely. By the spring of 1978, one battalion of the 2d Infantry Division had been withdrawn, accompanied by some support troops. Other units were expected to be withdrawn soon. On a positive note, however, Holbrooke's tactics were beginning to succeed. Congressional opposition to the ongoing pullout had grown, and such influential senators as Sam Nunn and John Glenn, both members of Carter's own Democratic Party, had expressed concern and reservations over the policy. Also, a bill providing large-scale arms assistance for the ROK, which was considered a prerequisite by the military for further U.S. troop withdrawals, was having difficulty in Congress, partly due to opposition to troop withdrawal itself but also because of anger over the alleged bribing of American officials by members of the Park government.[17] Finally, the army study sponsored by General Aaron had resulted in new appraisals by both the CIA and the DIA of North Korean forces. For the first time, these estimates were included in another Presidential Review Memorandum, PRM-45.

PRM-13, the original document by which Carter had officially declared his withdrawal policy, had been rushed through the government bureaucracy with only minimal consultation and review. By contrast, PRM-45, which would eventually be the document that halted the withdrawal, was widely circulated. PRM-45 was drafted in late 1978 and staffed in early 1979.[18] It was much more comprehensive than PRM-13, for it included extensive information on U.S. policy interests in Asia and Korea, the North-South military balance, the views of allies in the region such as Japan, and numerous other factors that Carter had not adequately considered and that had not been presented by his inexperienced staff during the early days of his presidency.

In the spring of 1979, USFK and the embassy in Seoul were finally formally consulted on troop reductions. Personnel there were presented with a draft of PRM-45, which was hand delivered to Seoul by the State Department's Korea desk officer, Bob Rich. Both General Vessey and the new ambassador, William H. Gleysteen Jr., were able to ensure that their views were incorporated into the final draft. Both opposed Carter's plans.

Soon after these consultations, there were some press reports speculating that Carter, who was scheduled to visit South Korea in late June, 1979, would announce the reversal of his troop-withdrawal policy at that time. These reports were false. Actually they were the result of leaks from the president's own staff, possibly the offices of Holbrooke and others who supported his views. These were designed to make it easier for the president to reverse himself, but the actual result was that he hardened his position. By this time almost all of Carter's senior advisers hoped he would reverse his withdrawal policy. This was even true of Secretaries Vance and Brown, although both men were reluctant to approach Carter on the issue. By the time of the president's trip to Korea, only Brzezinski and Carter himself still wanted to withdraw forces from the peninsula.

It was from the vantage point of Seoul that I observed the Carter visit and the denouement of the battle over troop withdrawal. During the summer of 1977, after completing my studies at the U.S. Army's Command and General Staff College at Fort Leavenworth, Kansas, I was selected as the army's first assistant military attaché to South Korea.

CHAPTER 4

To Korea Again

Previous to my assignment, there had been only a single military attaché at the U.S. Embassy in Seoul, and his duties had been largely ceremonial. In contrast, since the army had by now invested a considerable amount of time and training in developing my skills as a Korea expert, I was expected to function primarily as a reporting officer. My duties were to inform the U.S. Defense Intelligence Agency of all appropriate matters concerning the Korean military situation and to keep the Washington intelligence community informed on the Korean situation in general. My immediate boss was the embassy's defense attaché, but I was also expected to work closely with all other members of the embassy team, especially the Special Assistant's Office and Political Section, and with U.S. Forces Korea.

The Embassy Staff

The embassy in Seoul, like most embassies around the world, was organized around the "country team" concept. Each agency had its own representative who was responsible to report back to Washington items of interest to his particular agency or department and to serve as his department's representative to the government in Seoul. Accordingly, the commercial attaché reported to the Department of Commerce, the political counselor to the State Department, the defense attaché to the Defense Department, and so on. Each had their own staff and budget, and though they all were responsible to the ambassador as well, most tended to put the requirements of their home agency ahead of their embassy staff duties.

Nonetheless, the embassy functioned well, for the most part, without friction between its members. The State Department, which had the most staff members and therefore the most influence, tended to dominate some of the other sections, but the Defense Department and the Special Assistant's Office were both very strong in their own right. They had good support from their Washington headquarters, so their officers in Seoul tended to operate independently. The embassy sections with which I worked the closest were the Special Assistant's Office, the Political Section, and occasionally certain elements of the large USFK headquarters at Yongsan.

I occasionally saw Gen. John W. Vessey, the Central Forces Command–USFK commander, but was not a member of his staff, and thus most of my dealings were with his intelligence office, or J-2 section. William Clark, the embassy political counselor, was a professional diplomat and a solid if somewhat cautious operator who spent most of his time trying to sort out the complex political situation. He had no military experience and only a superficial knowledge of the ROK military. My immediate boss was Col. Don Blottie, who had no previous experience in Korea. He had been given the job as defense attaché in Seoul as a reward for his effective service as army attaché in Pakistan. Colonel Blottie was a fine gentleman and a very competent officer for whom I have always had much respect, but he was a little out of his element, with no language capability and no real training as a Korea specialist. The strongest of the senior embassy staff, in my opinion, was Bob Brewster, the special assistant to the ambassador. Brewster was a first-class gentleman and intelligence professional (CIA) who had experience all over the world. He had an excellent reputation in Washington, was well liked by the Koreans with whom he came in contact, and was admired and respected by his own staff. Ambassador William H. Gleysteen placed great faith in the capabilities and judgment of Brewster, who was to play a critical role in future events.

Because of the important part that the armed services played in South Korean politics at that time, Brewster had a keen interest in that nation's military affairs. He met with senior officers often, and we quickly developed a close personal and professional relationship. We traded information frequently and attended each other's social functions. Brewster's deputy for operational matters was a former U.S. Army Special Forces lieutenant colonel, who was also extremely competent. We became good friends and played golf together almost every weekend. By the summer of 1979, when the South Korean domestic situation began to deteriorate, we had solidified a relationship that allowed us to work closely together with mutual trust and personal compatibility.

Early Reporting on Chun Doo Hwan, Et Al.

One of the areas of mutual interest between the Defense Attaché Office and the Special Assistant's Office was in identifying and building information on the emerging leadership of the ROK Army. Although during my second stint in Korea the North Korean military situation was of importance, my duties also included monitoring the ROK military, which was heavily involved in political matters and thus both a source of and potential threat to internal stability. Because of this past work and because I had good relations and access to the Korean military, I now was given the responsibility to research and prepare a report that would identify the most likely future leaders.

My earlier job in this area had given me a good sense of the key personalities in the army—their likes and dislikes, their assignment histories, and their attitudes toward the United States. At the time the information was of a rather low priority in the overall intelligence picture, but it became useful when foreign officers were visiting their American counterparts or one of our senior officers was going on a trip overseas. Through my reading of many "bio" reports, I began to notice a pattern that convinced me there was a recognizable division between the older Korean generals and the younger officers. This split was sharpest between the generation of officers who had served in the Korean War and the group who had been trained at the four-year Korean Military Academy. It became evident that this latter group would be the predominant power in the ROK Army in a few years and that it would be in the interest of the United States to begin to cultivate close relations with the four-year KMA (Class 11 and below) group.

To most Koreans who were familiar with the ROK Army, these divisions were probably well known, but they were not to Americans. Despite the fact that the United States had maintained forces in South Korea for many years, only a few Americans understood the Korean Armed Forces in any detail. Most U.S. officers served in Korea only for one or two years and were more concerned with short-term issues than developing an understanding of their Korean counterparts. In addition, there were significant differences in the cultures of the two militaries. In the U.S. military, for example, the source of one's commission was of little importance. An ROTC graduate could reasonably expect to become a general or attain an equivalent rank on almost an equal basis with a graduate of West Point. The concept of family background was only of passing interest, and the region where one came from was unimportant. Officers from Texas, for example, might well have among their best friends officers from New York or California. Yet in the Korean military system, officers from one province tended to band together, and it was then almost unheard of for a non-KMA graduate to reach the highest ranks in the military. As a result of this cultural difference, most Americans tended to look at the Korean officers as "all the same," which was incorrect, of course.

I supplemented my prior knowledge with several weeks of additional research during early 1978 before submitting a lengthy report, a portion of which is paraphrased as follows:

> There is now a growing division in the ROK Army, which while not yet serious, may be so in the future. The senior leadership of the army, which is composed of those officers commissioned during the Korea War, is mostly from Class 7 and earlier. These officers will soon be leaving, but their departure will not significantly improve the promotion prospects for the youngest and perhaps most capable officers, those from Class 11 and later. These officers, who are only now reaching General officer rank, are increasingly frustrated. They see themselves as better educated, more seasoned, and more modern in their outlook and behavior than their predecessors, yet the path to the top is blocked.
>
> Most of the Class 11 and later groups' frustration is aimed at Class 8. This group, many of whom have been General Officers for many years, is well organized and powerful. Their primary sponsor is Kim Jong Pil, and they are presently concentrated at the two-star level. The Class 11 and younger group sees Class 8 as a direct challenge and impediment to their career progression. If they are forced to wait until this group has had its opportunity to lead the army, they will be approaching normal retirement age without having the chance to reach their full potential. This factor alone seems to indicate that there will ultimately have to be a solution to this issue.

Another section of the report read: "There are several leaders of the Class 11 group who will likely play a major role in this process. Major General Chun Doo Hwan, presently commanding the 1st ROK Division near Munsan is one. Others include his classmates Roh Tae Woo and Chung Ho Young. As the leaders of the four-year KMA graduates, this group bears responsibility to see that those who follow them, and themselves, of course, are treated fairly in the future promotion process."

This report was widely read and well received among the embassy staff and in Washington. Bob Brewster took particular interest in it, as did his staff. We also received several written evaluations from Washington on this report, indicating that it had been of the highest value. After the events of December, 1979 (to be described in the next chapter), I was very surprised when officials in Washington and later in Seoul claimed to have no knowledge or biographical information on Chun Doo Hwan, who they referred to as a "previously unknown officer." He was indeed quite well known, especially within the intelligence community, and had associated with embassy officers such as Colonel Hiebert for at least eight years.

Activities of Other Military Attachés

My duties also included maintaining liaison with the other military attachés from various countries assigned to Korea. There were about twenty other countries that had such officers accredited to Seoul, and we met together frequently. Most of this contact was social, for few of the other attachés had much interest in the Korean situation and were involved more in representational duties such as social events and parades than in the substance of the military situation. There were, however, two exceptions. Both the German attaché and the Japanese attaché worked very hard to understand the situation, particularly after October, when President Park was assassinated. The Japanese Army attaché was Col. Ahiro Hagino, who was very competent, spoke excellent Korean, and had a strong background in Korean military and political affairs. He later became a three-star general and after retirement continued to work closely with Korea as a businessman. I had great respect for Colonel Hagino's professional capabilities, having worked with him several years before while on the Northeast Asia Desk in Washington. I had better sources of information on North Korea, but I rated his knowledge of South Korea as equal to my own. During the crisis period of late 1979 and 1980, we would see much of each other as we attempted to piece together the true picture of events.

Denouement of the Troop-Withdrawal Issue

The most momentous event of my third tour in Korea prior to the assassination of President Park was President Carter's visit in late June, 1978. By that time we were reasonably hopeful that Carter would reverse his policy on troop withdrawal. We had busied ourselves with plans for the visit for many weeks in anticipation that its outcome might have a substantial influence on policy.[1]

Carter landed in Seoul on June 29 and immediately helicoptered to Camp Casey near the DMZ, where he was briefed by General Vessey and mingled with American troops of the 2d Division. He did not meet President Park until the next day, and their first encounter was nearly a disaster. Against strong U.S. advice, Park began the meeting by sternly admonishing his guest on his withdrawal policy.[2] Carter, who had a bad impression of Park to begin with based on his human rights record and military background, grew angry with the lengthy lecture. His jaw grew tense, and at one time he grew so angry that he considered threatening to remove *all* U.S. forces from Korea if Park continued. This meeting did nothing to improve the situation.

The two presidents then met privately for a few minutes, but again without any improvement in the atmosphere; if anything, their mutual distrust only increased. When word of this calamity reached us in the embassy, we were afraid that all the carefully laid plans of PRM-45 and the long efforts to change President Carter's mind had been in vain.

Upon returning from the unpleasant confrontation at the Blue House, Secretaries Vance and Brown, National Security Adviser Brzezinski, and Ambassador Gleysteen rode in the same large limousine with President Carter. After reaching the ambassador's residence, where several embassy staffers, including myself, and some press were waiting, the car stopped, but no one got out (greatly frustrating the aide whose job, rehearsed often over the preceding days, was to open the president's automobile door). Inside the car there was a heated discussion. Carter directly asked each of his top advisers if they disagreed with his policy. At first nobody replied. Sensing that his top advisers were reluctant to disagree with Carter, Ambassador Gleysteen finally took the initiative. "Yes, Mr. President, I disagree," he said. He then explained directly to Carter's face why he thought the policy was wrong, citing factors such as the overall U.S. commitment to security in East Asia, the effect withdrawal would have on Japan, Chinese concerns, and other major diplomatic factors. After he finished, Vance and Brown, who by now had been convinced by their staffs that withdrawal was not a good idea, supported Gleysteen's remarks. Only Brzezinski remained silent.[3]

From this point on, the American side was engaged at putting the best possible face on the earlier meeting with President Park. We redrafted the joint ROK-U.S. communiqué, emphasizing the points on which the two presidents had agreed and purposely leaving out the several points of disagreement. Secretaries Vance and Brown, accompanied by Ambassador Gleysteen, paid official calls on their Korean counterparts, trying to play down any damage done by the presidential meetings and to ensure that there would be smooth interaction between Park and Carter during that evening's state dinner. This effort succeeded, and the state dinner went off without a hitch.

By the time Carter and his entourage left Seoul on July 1, we had managed to put a reasonably positive face on the visit for the public, but we were not at all certain that Carter would finally relent on troop withdrawal. Many Koreans and Americans believe that the trip to Korea changed Carter's mind on the issue, but in fact it almost had had the opposite effect. Ambassador Gleysteen's frank talk and the excellent staff work that had been done on PRM-45 in Washington helped save the day. Apparently, though, so did President Park's private assurances to Carter that he would increase ROK defense spending beyond 6 percent of the country's gross national product and make some positive moves on human rights. Only days after Carter's departure, Park informed Gleysteen that over the next six months he would release 180 political prisoners.

On his return to Washington, Carter was overwhelmed by other issues. Follow-up action on the Korea trip was delegated to others. PRM-45 was eventually approved by the president in late July, if still reluctantly. The actual decision as publicly announced was to temporarily "suspend" the troop withdrawal pending "further review," but this was just face-saving rhetoric. The Carter plan was dead. It was perhaps fitting that the official announcement of the policy change was made by National Security Adviser Brzezinski, who had been the last holdout favoring withdrawal.[4]

The Looming Storm

By the late summer and fall of 1979, political unrest in South Korea had reached new heights. Student demonstrations, labor unrest and dissatisfaction, and the mysterious death of a student in the Pusan area had fueled large demonstrations against the government. The U.S. Embassy viewed these protests seriously and took efforts to encourage the Korean government to treat the demonstrators with more compassion and less force. The embassy was particularly concerned that military forces might have to be used to augment the police if the demonstrations got out of control, and it wanted to avoid direct conflict between government forces and citizens if at all possible. This was the message emphasized to the Park government at every opportunity, but it did not seem to have much effect. Even in those cases where senior ROK government officials were sympathetic, they were either afraid to stand up to the Blue House or were blocked in their efforts to urge a more conciliatory policy. Among the hard-liners appeared to be Cha Chi Chol, the Blue House secretary, or chief of staff, who had a great influence over direct access to President Park and what information he received. Since military affairs were my department, most of my knowledge of what was transpiring between the embassy and the Seoul government on this political issue came secondhand. I do know, however, that the embassy's Political Section was very concerned about the situation and was trying hard to convince the Blue House to take a softer approach.[5]

On October 25 I drove to Chinhae on the south coast of Korea west of Pusan to visit our three foreign-area officers, who were attending the ROK Army Staff College and were under my supervision. I received briefings on their training progress and some routine administrative matters, spending the evening of the twenty-sixth at dinner with a friend, Mike Eggerman. Early on the morning of October 27, I was awakened by Maj. Ash Ormes, one of our three students, to receive the news that President Park had been shot the previous evening. A new and critical stage in the relationship between the United States and South Korea was about to begin.

CHAPTER 5

The Park Assassination
and Its Aftermath

I returned to Seoul and the U.S. Embassy as soon as possible, arriving early on the afternoon of October 27, 1979, and went directly to my office. Col. Don Blottie was there and had attended several meetings that morning with the senior embassy staff. He told me that our staff had been shocked and concerned and was still putting together all the details and known facts concerning the assassination. He said that Pres. Park Chung Hee had been killed by the South Korean CIA director, Kim Jae Kyu, and that the internal situation was as calm as could be expected under the circumstances. The purpose of the several meetings at the embassy and the military headquarters at Yongsan was to assess the situation, particularly as it concerned North Korea. The primary concern was clearly to ensure that the North not take advantage of the situation. There also had been some concern about a coup attempt by the military in view of the power vacuum created by Park's death, but those fears had apparently evaporated.

Even though most people had speculated as to what might happen if President Park should die suddenly or decide to step down, the embassy and the U.S. government were completely unprepared for the actual event. Unlike the Korean government, which had prepared contingency plans and immediately declared martial law, the Americans had no idea how to proceed. After consultations with Washington and the local meetings, the State Department decided to issue a statement: "The United States Government wishes to make it clear that it will react strongly in accordance with its treaty obligations to the Republic of Korea to any external attempt to exploit the situation in the Republic of Korea."[1] The military thought that more concrete steps should be taken, a view supported by the Defense Department. This resulted in the deployment of a naval task force, increasing the readiness posture of our forces in Korea and some air force units in the region, and deploying Airborne Warning and Control System (AWACS) aircraft to the area in order to better monitor North Korean military activities.

In the days and even years that followed, some Koreans believed that either the U.S. government, or the American CIA, had some role in the assassination of President Park. I have never, in all my time spent in the Korean intelligence business, found even the most remote evidence of this. It is true that Park was not very popular in Washington, especially after Carter became president. Nonetheless, involvement in Park's assassination by the Carter administration would have been completely out of character. In fact, at the time of Park's death, the Carter administration was taking strong and decisive actions to reduce the CIA's capabilities, especially in the clandestine operations area. Also, CIA involvement in assassinations was at the time (and still is) prohibited by U.S. law. The political climate in Washington in 1979 was such that it would have been impossible to conduct such an operation in secret.[2]

A few days after the assassination, I personally reviewed most of the intelligence reporting and cable messages in the days leading up to Park's death and could find no evidence that would lead a reasonable person to conclude that he was in any physical danger. There were, however, some indications that moderates in the Korean government felt Park was taking too firm a posture regarding student and labor demonstrations. There was also some reporting that indicated frustration because access to the president was so tightly controlled, especially by his universally disliked chief of staff, Cha Chi Chol, who was assassinated as well. In retrospect, I believe that Cha's heavy-handed and arrogant behavior was at least partially responsible for President Park's assassination. But I am totally convinced that the United States neither had a role in it nor had any reason to suspect foul play in advance.

In the days that followed, U.S. government policy toward Korea focused on two major objectives. The first was ensuring that the North Koreans would not try to take advantage of the situation. This was accomplished by increasing our surveillance of the North, particularly their communications transmissions, and by conducting frequent satellite observation of their military forces. After a few days it was evident that the North was taking no unusual actions, but we continued to closely monitor the situation.

The second objective was to encourage political reform. Some State Department officers in Washington believed that the death of Park could open the way for progress on democracy, human rights, and the overall political reforms that were of such importance to the administration. Carter selected Secretary of State Vance as his personal representative at Park's funeral, and Vance indicated the importance of political reform during a press conference in Washington prior to his departure for Seoul: "We hope that political growth in the Republic of Korea will be commensurate with economic and social progress."[3] He later discussed the importance that the administration placed on these issues with Pres. Choi Kyu Ha, Park's successor, urging the release of certain political prisoners and efforts to form a truly representative and democratic government in South Korea such as direct election of the president and a revised constitution.[4]

While Vance's remarks were well meaning, it was obvious to even the most unsophisticated observer that the focus of power in South Korea remained with the military. Yet the State Department and the U.S. Embassy felt they had no real choice but to deal with the legal government of President Choi, who, although first in the line of succession to Park under the Yushin Constitution, was a career bureaucrat with weak credentials for top leadership. U.S. diplomats ignored the opportunity to expand direct contacts with the ROK military, seeking instead to use every opportunity to convince the Choi government to make sweeping changes even though it had no real power to do so. Some of us believed that a better choice would have been to accept the power situation as it really existed by opening up a more direct channel. It was clear that under martial law Choi was only a figurehead. Even after martial law was lifted, the military would still hold the ultimate political power. Yet the State Department continued to play the charade that it was making progress on the political reform issue through the "legitimate authorities."

Chung Sung Hwa

During the period immediately following Park's death, ROK Army chief of staff Gen. Chung Sung Hwa was involved in great controversy because of his presence at a dinner party on the same compound and near the location where the president was assassinated. As the facts emerged, however, his role appeared to be one of innocence in the assassination plot, more a victim of circumstance. Under the declaration of martial law, he was the commander, with significant authority that went well beyond his normal military duties.

The U.S. military-intelligence community's appraisal of General Chung was quite favorable. He had a reputation as a competent officer and was considered to be more sophisticated, polished, and open to fresh ideas than most of his contemporaries. Chung had been somewhat of a surprise choice as army chief of staff since he had been the First ROK Army commander, usually considered less prestigious than some other four-star positions such as command of the Third ROK Army. He had a reputation as a thoughtful, well-read, nonpolitical, and conservative officer. Although his views of the internal Korean political situation were not well known, he appeared to be more moderate than most of his fellow generals.[5] Considering his powerful position, I recommended to Bob Brewster that a direct channel be established with General Chung. In this way the embassy might be able to make its views known and have some success at having those views implemented during the transition, particularly concerning political reform. As it was, the constant urging of the embassy at the "official" levels achieved nothing other than polite listening.

Brewster agreed with my idea, and we began to make initial plans to implement it after coordination with the Political Section and the ambassador. We were both enthusiastic about the plan, which might have held out real hope for the advancement of democracy in South Korea and also avoided subsequent events, including the December 12 army coup of Maj. Gen. Chun Doo Hwan, the imposition of martial law in May, 1980, and the Kwangju incident.[6] Unfortunately the plan was disapproved after objections by the Political Section, objections supported by the ambassador.

Why was this initiative never carried out? I think for three reasons. First, General Chung was personally involved in the events surrounding President Park's death. There was concern that close cooperation and contact with him would fuel the speculation that the United States was somehow involved in the assassination. Rumors of U.S. involvement were sweeping Seoul at that time, and the Political Section did not want to make them any more credible than necessary. Second, our plan called for using the intelligence channel rather than the diplomatic channel. The State Department was likely concerned that it would lose control of what it viewed as an essentially political matter. Of course, the reality of the time was that political and military matters were almost one in the same, but this was a moot point. Third, some of the State Department's foreign-service officers had an almost paranoid distrust of the military, and they feared U.S. association with martial law in the eyes of the Korean public. Few of them had ever served on active duty, and those who had were not fond of the experience. They believed that everyone in the ROK military thought the same way, that they were interested only in staying in power, and that they would never agree to liberalizing the political system. This was incorrect—some of the military men thought that way, but others did not. I believed that General Chung was a reasonable man with whom we could have strong dialogue and direct, continuing contact. But it was not to be. A channel to the military moderates was never opened.

During this period between the 10/26 and 12/12 incidents (Park's assassination and Chun's military coup respectively—major events in Korea are frequently referred to by the numbers of their month and day), there were a lot of rumors flying around Seoul, and it was often difficult to separate truth from fiction. Consistently, however, we began to receive reports of dissatisfaction from some elements of the military about the role of General Chung in the Park assassination. Since Chung was the army chief of staff and martial-law commander, it was very difficult to conduct an in-depth investigation of his actions. His explanations had seemed satisfactory to most of us, and his actions following the assassination, including the arrest of ROK CIA Chief Kim Jae Kyu, seemed proper and appropriate. Nonetheless, there were some signs that Chun Doo Hwan, who was by this time head of the Defense Security Command (DSC) and thus had the authority under martial law to investigate such matters, was coming under pressure to investigate more closely the general's role in the murder.

In addition to these reports, there were indications that Chung was aware of the possibility that he might be under some continued scrutiny by the DSC. In those days the DSC was greatly feared and had agents in every military unit. While their official purpose was to ensure adequate "security," these operatives were in reality political watchdogs whose agency was independent of the normal military chain of command. The DSC commander was traditionally chosen by the president himself, and Park had used the agency as his eyes and ears to watch the military and prevent any coup attempts. Under martial law as it existed in November and early December, 1979, the DSC was even more powerful.

I believe that General Chung was aware that General Chun might move against him. He appeared to take extra security precautions at times, and these were explained away by his aides because of martial law and Chung's need for extra protection as commander. In retrospect, however, he needed more security than he had.

In late November or early December, we began to receive reports that there would be some reassignments within the army. December was usually the time when routine military reassignments were announced, but this year we had expected normal reassignments to be delayed because of the uncertain situation. One rumor was that Chung intended to reassign Chun Doo Hwan from Seoul to the East Coast Security Command headquartered near Sokcho. If true, it would be perceived as removing Chun from the scene because of his powerful and dangerous (to Chung) position as DSC commander. Regardless, the reassignment would mean the effective end of Chun's career in the army. But if U.S. military intelligence knew that Chun might be transferred, Chun himself would also know it; after all, he had many DSC field agents reporting to him, especially from within army headquarters.

About the same time, our Political Section received a cable from the State Department. According to the message, a Japanese diplomat in Washington had been discussing the Korean situation with his American counterpart, and the Japanese Foreign Ministry was of the opinion that Chun Doo Hwan was the most important and powerful figure in South Korea because of his authority to investigate others as DSC commander under martial law. The underlying tone of this message was simple: "be careful of Chun!"

One of the junior officers from the Political Section had brought this message down to see if the Defense Attaché Office had any information on Chun. After I finished laughing, I gave the officer a briefing on what we already knew. After he left I began to wonder whether the left hand knew what the right hand was doing—obviously we were in big trouble if Washington had such a superficial understanding of the situation that it did not know who Chun was, especially after all the reporting we had done. The problem was that, while the DIA and CIA obviously had large amounts of information, the State Department, at least at the working levels, was only peripherally aware of this important personality. Soon they would recognize his name quite well.

Other Indications of Developing Trouble

To this point, I have focused primarily on the activities within the U.S. Embassy and in Washington. There was also significant information available within the U.S. military headquarters at Yongsan. The Combined Forces Command (CFC) was a binational (Korean and American) organization with the straightforward mission of deterring attack by external forces and, if deterrence failed, to defend the ROK. Unlike the embassy, which had a political and reporting mission, CFC was focused entirely on its military mission. U.S. Forces Korea, however, was a unilateral, U.S.-only headquarters, and within that organization were military-intelligence units. Some of these worked closely in a liaison role with various ROK intelligence agencies. These sources also were picking up the same information that we had reported. Specifically they were aware that there was speculation that General Chun might be reassigned to the East Coast Security Command and that he was under pressure to interrogate Chung Sung Wha concerning his role in the 10/26 incident. This information was forwarded through army channels and was routinely available throughout the Washington intelligence community, including the DIA, CIA, and State Department. The embassy also received these reports, but I am not aware that there was ever any concern shown or action taken as a result. Gen. John Wickham, who had recently replaced General Vessey as the senior American military commander in Korea, was personally aware of these reports and of growing unrest among the four-year Korean Military Academy group led by Chun, and I suspect that Ambassador Gleysteen was aware of them as well.[7] In fact, several years later it was officially revealed that General Wickham had actually discussed these reports with his deputy CFC commander, Gen. Lew Byong Hyun, and other senior ROK defense officials, including Defense Minister Rho Jae Hyun, but that the consensus was that these reports were not credible.[8]

At this time I was meeting regularly with the Japanese attaché. He was hearing the same stories as the USFK intelligence units and myself and was of the opinion that South Korea was approaching a crisis period. He was convinced that Chun was in a very strong position and, if ordered to leave his Seoul DSC posting for the east coast, would refuse. Throughout this period, I was of the opinion that the Japanese knew more than they were telling, that they had excellent information on the situation, possibly better than we had.

Looking back on all of this, it is difficult to believe that we missed anticipating the 12/12 incident, or at least something similar to it. I am still not sure why, but one possible explanation is that the embassy staff was concentrating on other issues and considered these reports as military matters, while the military was focused on watching North Korea. USFK as an institution also had a natural dislike for investigating such reports in any depth because they were considered internal ROK Army matters. General Wickham likely believed that he had done his duty by bringing the reports to the attention of his Korean counterparts, especially Minister Rho and General Lew. When they showed no concern he was satisfied.[9]

In fact, had General Wickham been in his job longer and had time to develop a better feel for the Korean military, he would have known that Minister Rho was held in almost universal disdain, especially by those from Class 11 and later classes of the KMA. He was less well trained and less intelligent in their view—a perfect example of the "old school military." Their nickname for him (behind his back, obviously) was "Sergeant" Rho. He was a prime target for removal. As for General Lew, most serious Korea watchers believed the deputy CFC was generally chosen for his English-language skills and ability to get along well with the Americans rather than for any special capability or competence. Interestingly Lew later became a spokesman and apologist for Chun Doo Hwan. He was promoted to chairman of the ROK Joint Chiefs of Staff and later to the post of South Korean ambassador to the United States under the Chun regime. Had Wickham taken his information directly to General Chung, or had Brewster done so, the army chief of staff might not have been caught by surprise on December 12.

In the days leading up to the 12/12 incident, despite the tension in the air, the diplomatic circuit continued to host the usual rounds of official parties and receptions. It was often difficult to find a free night, one when some official function was not scheduled. I had recently been promoted to lieutenant colonel and was expected to host a promotion party to celebrate the occasion. After checking all available dates, we decided that the best one, when our Korean military friends would not be engaged, would be December 12, 1979. As it turned out, of course, they were actually very engaged that night.

CHAPTER 6

The 12/12 Incident

Entertainment customs of the South Korean military and Western countries were somewhat different. Most Western countries include wives in their social events, while most Korean parties are for men only. We decided that my promotion party would follow the Korean military custom since most of the guests were Korean. We gathered at my quarters, which were located at Yongsan South Post in the U.S. Embassy housing area. Most of the residences were duplexes, but mine was a single-family house. Like the others, however, it was of cinder-block construction. Though dated, it was nicely furnished due to the requirement to entertain frequently.

The party was very well attended, including several ROK officers at the two- and three-star level. This was quite an honor for me since I was only a brand-new lieutenant colonel. Also attending were many of the military attachés, a few representatives of U.S. Forces Korea, and some members of the embassy staff, including Bob Brewster and Col. Don Blottie. The party began at about 6:00 P.M. and was great fun, with a lot of the camaraderie that is typical of military gatherings. I spent much of the time making certain that my guests were comfortable but also talking to Lieutenant General Chong, who was commandant of the ROK Marine Corps, and Maj. Gen. Choi Sung Taek, who was the senior ROK Army-intelligence officer present. A little later General Choi was called away rather abruptly. I walked him to his car, bid farewell, and returned to my guests. It was evident from his manner and the fact that he was talking on his radio net that something unusual was happening, but at that time I had no indication that it was a really serious incident.[1]

I returned to my guests for a few more minutes, but they gradually began to depart. Among the last to leave were General Chong and Bob Brewster. About two minutes after the last guest left, the telephone rang. This call was from a Korean officer who was very excited. He said that there were reports of ROK Army units moving and that there had been some sort of incident at the official residence of the army chief of staff, Gen. Chung

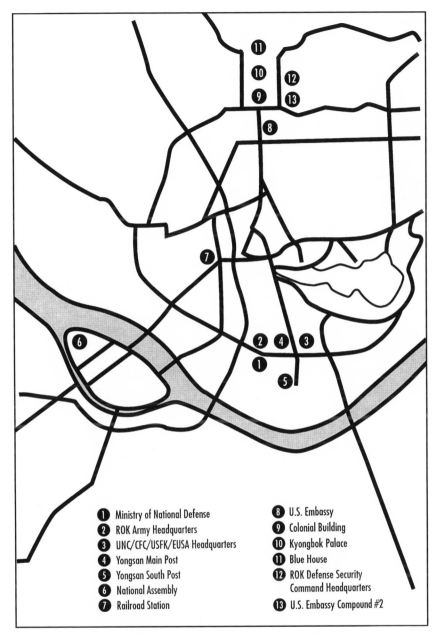

1. Ministry of National Defense
2. ROK Army Headquarters
3. UNC/CFC/USFK/EUSA Headquarters
4. Yongsan Main Post
5. Yongsan South Post
6. National Assembly
7. Railroad Station
8. U.S. Embassy
9. Colonial Building
10. Kyongbok Palace
11. Blue House
12. ROK Defense Security Command Headquarters
13. U.S. Embassy Compound #2

Map 2. Central Seoul on December 12, 1979. Map drawn by Wendy Giminski, Campus Graphics and Photography Department, University of Georgia.

Sung Hwa. The caller asked if I knew any more details, which, of course, I did not. I hung up the phone but it rang again immediately. This time it was a call for Brewster from his duty officer, who urgently requested to talk to him. I explained that he had just left and was probably en route to his home at the embassy compound number two, near Kwanghwamun. Just after I hung up, the phone rang once again. This time it was Brewster's deputy, who also asked for Bob. We discussed briefly what we knew about the situation, which was not much. Since normal procedure was to report to the Yongsan bunker in the case of an emergency, we decided to go there immediately.

In the Bunker

The USFK command bunker was located only about five minutes from my residence. When I arrived there were only a few officers present, together with the normal "watch" personnel whose duties were to observe and track the military situation twenty-four hours a day. To my knowledge, General Wickham and Ambassador William Gleysteen arrived about the same time and went to a separate section of the bunker.

The Yongsan bunker was somewhat old and outdated compared with the more technically sophisticated facilities now used. A portion of the bunker was devoted to office space, but the important sections were the operations and intelligence center and a separate section toward the rear, which was normally reserved for senior commanders and staff. The operations and intelligence center contained the "Red" North Korea forces display and was the place where all intelligence relating to these forces was gathered, analyzed, and acted upon as necessary. The other room held the "Blue," or friendly, forces information and contained a large map of the DMZ.

Upon arrival I talked for a few moments with the watch officer, primarily to determine if there was any unusual activity going on in North Korea. He replied that there was not, that everything was normal but that our forces were increasing their watchfulness because of the confusing situation in Seoul. I then called Colonel Blottie, alerted him to the situation, and recommended that he report to the bunker as soon as possible.

When Blottie arrived, I briefed him on the situation as we knew it, which was that there were some ROK troop movements, the details of which were still unclear, that Chun Doo Hwan had apparently arrested Chung Sung Hwa, and that in my judgment there was likely some sort of military coup occurring. We then entered the special separate section of the bunker in order to provide staff support to Ambassador Gleysteen and to see what other information was available concerning the situation. At this time Bob Brewster also arrived and accompanied us into the rear room.

In this room were Ambassador Gleysteen; General Wickham; Major General Prillaman, who was the J-3, or plans and operations, chief; General Wickham's aide; and Brewster, Blottie, and myself. Also present was Gen. Lew Byong Hyun, who was the deputy commander of Combined Forces Command. At the main table Ambassador Gleysteen and General Wickham sat side by side, and General Lew sat opposite, facing them. Major General Prillaman stood at the large map, which contained the positions of ROK forces. The rest of us sat behind the main table. No one else was present.[2]

Neither General Wickham nor Ambassador Gleysteen had a clear picture of the situation. In fact, everyone present appeared confused. Wickham was asking questions of Lew, and Prillaman was on the telephone attempting to find out the situation involving those ROK forces assigned to guard Seoul and the critical attack corridors along the DMZ. Gradually they began putting together what had happened. Wickham seemed concerned that there would be an attempt by Chun to physically seize the Blue House or the Ministry of National Defense (MND), and quite a bit of time was spent studying special maps of these areas. Also, there were reports of Korean military units fighting each other; these reports continued coming in throughout the night. Later we determined that these accounts were untrue and were in most cases only retellings of the shooting incident at General Chung's residence when he was arrested. At the time, however, the situation appeared to be much worse than it actually was—we learned later that, while several individuals were indeed shot, including the Special Forces commander and the capital defense commander, the stories about actual battles between South Korean units were exaggerated. General Wickham took the lead in directing activity since both he and the ambassador felt this was primarily a military situation. He had an immediate objective: to ensure that there were as few friendly casualties as possible, that ROK forces not fight themselves. Unfortunately he was unable to make contact with any of the Korean forces involved despite several attempts to contact Chun Doo Hwan directly. This was either due to the chaotic situation or was a deliberate desire of Chun to avoid contact with the U.S. side until he had complete control of the situation. Later General Wickham did have some success by persuading forces loyal to Chung Sung Hwa to suspend their movement, but he was never able to get through to Chun. He also ordered increased surveillance of North Korea by our intelligence units, for both he and

Ambassador Gleysteen were concerned that the North might try to take advantage of the situation.

General Wickham was especially surprised and incensed at the movement of CFC forces during the night, particularly those assigned to sensitive DMZ duty. At one point he called the American three-star commander at Uijongbu to confirm that Korean troops under his operational control had moved without notification. After checking with his ROK Army counterparts, the Uijongbu commander initially reported that all forces were in place. This was not true, of course, and it left General Wickham with a false impression of the actual situation. A short time later this report was changed to state that several units had indeed moved toward the Seoul area. Normally a mild-mannered and controlled person, Wickham's face grew red, and he was visibly angered as the truth of these reports became evident.

To this point the embassy staff and ambassador had been primarily observers. Ambassador Gleysteen had earlier tried to reach President Choi by telephone, though without success. He now called the State Department for "consultations" and was on the phone several times with Assistant Secretary of State Richard Holbrooke.

The primary diplomatic concern was that the power play by Chun would set back the democratization process. The State Department was also concerned about civil unrest and even civil war in the ROK, not to mention the possibility that North Korea would try to take advantage of the situation. After several consultations, a statement was drafted as follows:

> During the past few weeks we had been encouraged by the orderly procedures adopted in the Republic of Korea to develop a broadly based government following the assassination of President Park. As a result of events today in Korea we have instructed our Ambassador and the Commander of U.S. Forces in Korea to point out to all concerned that any forces within the Republic of Korea which disrupt this progress should bear in mind the seriously adverse impact their actions would have on the ROK's relations with the United States. At the same time, any forces outside the ROK which might seek to exploit the current situation in Seoul should bear in mind our warning of October 27.[3]

From a practical standpoint, this statement had almost no effect. Since the embassy had no control over the local media, which were controlled by the ROK military, the only course of action was to release the statement in Washington. Few if any people in Seoul were ever aware of the position of the U.S. government, a condition that would continue and even grow worse during the days ahead. Indeed, to the average Korean, it even appeared that the United States was actually favoring the renegade generals since there was no evidence of disapproval expressed in the Korean media.

By now it was becoming obvious that there was very little new information coming into the bunker because of the lack of communication with ROK forces. I proposed to Colonel Blottie that I personally investigate the situation at the Ministry of Defense and perhaps the Blue House as well and then send a report to our Washington headquarters. He agreed and I prepared to depart.

I left the room just as ROK minister of defense Rho Jae Hyun and Joint Chiefs of Staff chairman Gen. Kim Chong Hwan entered the bunker. They both were pale and nervous; General Kim walked in front of Minister Rho, which was unusual. They entered the situation room and joined General Wickham and the ambassador, spending most of the rest of the evening trying to contact units loyal to MND. To my knowledge, this was only partially successful, and Minister Rho eventually decided to return to MND. General Wickham and Ambassador Gleysteen both objected strenuously to this idea out of concern for Roh's safety and a feeling that he would probably be captured or arrested if he left the USFK bunker. As it turned out, he was unharmed but was later persuaded to sign a statement authorizing the arrest of Chung Sung Hwa almost twelve hours after the actual event had taken place. Rho resigned the following day.

When I departed the bunker for MND, the roads were almost deserted. It was possible to drive past the MND building, but the entrances were blocked by soldiers and combat vehicles. I was told to leave immediately by a young soldier who looked like he meant business, and I complied. Driving north toward Seoul Station, I took note of the bumper numerals on the vehicles. ROK Army units, unlike their American counterparts, which had their unit designation printed on their vehicles, used a numbered code. Fortunately I knew the code for most of the major ROK units and could quickly ascertain that these vehicles were from a CFC front-line division. I reported this information to the bunker via my car radio and continued downtown toward the embassy.

On arrival near the embassy, I decided to see if there was any unusual military activity in the Blue House vicinity, but the normal entrance was blocked. This was not unusual, of course, since security around the Blue House was always tight, but that night the security appeared greater than usual. I then drove to the Kwanghwamun area, but instead of turning back toward the embassy, I decided at the last minute to drive by the area of Gen. Chun Doo Hwan's Defense Security Command headquarters.

This was a big mistake. The area was heavily guarded, with armored vehicles and even tanks around. I was stopped by two armed guards in full combat gear and told quite clearly to leave the area immediately. As I turned around I was greatly surprised to see the Japanese attaché walking rapidly from the area of the roadblock back toward his embassy. We did not have a chance to stop and talk, but seeing him convinced me again that the Japanese must have had excellent sources of information and probably knew as much or more about the situation as we did.

My job as an attaché was to report to the Defense Intelligence Agency and the Defense Department items of military significance. We now had unfolding probably the most important event involving the Korean military in almost twenty years, and although the State Department was being informed and USFK was in continuing contact with the operational chain of command, nothing had as yet come through my channel. My headquarters would be expecting information from the attaché office soon, so I went to the embassy and called in a telephonic report to the National Military Intelligence Center. I then prepared a follow-up written report, which is partially paraphrased as follows:

On the evening of December 12, Army Chief of Staff and Martial Law Commander General Chung Sung Hwa was arrested by forces under the control of DSC Commander Major General Chun Doo Hwan. There was fighting during the arrest, which occurred at the Chief of Staff's official residence, and some casualties resulted. Chung is presently in custody and is allegedly being questioned in connection with his role during the Presidential assassination of 10/26. There have also been significant troop movements by forces loyal to both the Chief of Staff and General Chun. Some of these forces appear to be units under the OPCON [operational control] of CFC, and include elements of several front-line divisions. These activities appear to be restricted to Army units; there is no indication of Air Force or Navy involvement.

As of 0500 local time, we cannot confirm further clashes between ROK Army units but believe the worst is behind us. Visual inspection of areas surrounding DSC Headquarters and MND confirm combat troop presence and armored vehicles. Blue House appears normal. Embassy and USFK are reporting events as they happen in their channels.

If Chun and his followers are successful, and it now appears that they have been, they are in a position to take effective control of the Army. The next few days will be instructive. If Chun moves to remove those officers senior to Class 11, particularly those from Class 8 which form the majority group which is now blocking the advancement of his followers from Class 11 and below, then the Army will be consolidated under his control. The political implications of this move are obviously significant, and we will continue to report accordingly.

I left this report with a clerk to type and transmit to our Washington headquarters, then returned to the Yongsan bunker.

By the time I returned it was almost dawn, and the atmosphere at the bunker had changed dramatically. General Wickham and Ambassador Gleysteen had departed and would be consulting with their senior staffs later that morning to decide on a future course of action. By now almost everyone realized that Chun Doo Hwan had been successful and that his move had greater ramifications for the future since he had taken effective control of the army. Whether he intended to use this new power for political purposes was still open to debate and would remain so for several months. The "Night of the Generals" had ended, and for all the concern expressed and effort expended by the American side, it was apparent that we had had little influence on the outcome.

The U.S. Role

In the days following the 12/12 incident, some Koreans wondered what the U.S. role had been. Specifically, questions were asked about our prior knowledge and why our sophisticated intelligence capability could not observe the movement of the ROK Army forces that had illegally participated in that incident. My opinion on these questions is as follows.

Simply stated, we had no prior knowledge that a coup was imminent, though perhaps we should have. Certainly we had information regarding the pressure on Chun to show some progress in the investigation of President Park's assassination, particularly concerning the continued suspicions about Chung Sung Hwa's actions. We also had received reports about the possibility of Chun Doo Hwan being reassigned to the east coast, which would have removed him from the army's power center. With considerable hindsight, one can argue that we should have suspected some sort of action by Chun.

But South Korean authorities had this information as well and considerably more resources with which to influence the situation, yet they also failed to prevent the coup of 12/12. Furthermore, when General Wickham raised the issue of unrest and discontent among Class 11 and Class 12 officers with Minister Rho and General Lew earlier, they did not take the reports seriously. However much I regret the failure of American officials to communicate directly with General Chung, I believe it would be unfair, considering all available information, to have expected us to either predict or prevent those events. In the final analysis, Chun and his followers were better prepared to carry out the 12/12 coup than General Chung and the existing authorities were to prevent it. That is the ultimate reason for its success.

During the 1988 National Assembly investigations of the 12/12 incident and the suppression of the Kwangju uprising of May, 1980, it was suggested that the U.S. intelligence network in Korea, particularly reconnaissance aircraft, should have detected the movement of CFC forces in the first case. This is ridiculous. First, our intelligence resources in Korea in 1979–80, as they are today, were focused on North Korea, not South Korea. Second, these actions happened suddenly and at night, which increased the difficulty of detecting them even if they had been a matter of prior concern. In fact, the American side was not even certain of exactly which ROK Army units were actually involved until two or three days later, when the whole story was reconstructed. Third, we had no reason to suspect that CFC forces would be moved illegally. It had never happened before, and such a thing is so foreign and unbelievable to most U.S. officers that even today most of us who were personally involved in these events still cannot forget the betrayal by our ROK Army counterparts. Fortunately the CFC structure is now stronger and the South Korean Army much less politically oriented, so perhaps the real legacy of 12/12 is that it eventually resulted in a stronger CFC and a better professional relationship between the American and Korean military.

Effect of 12/12 on the ROK-U.S. Relationship

Despite the good professional relationship today, the immediate effect of 12/12 on the ROK-U.S. military relationship in 1979–80 was to greatly diminish the respect we had previously held for our Korean comrades in arms. It left General Wickham and his staff suspicious of their counterparts and reduced the general's own credibility in Washington. In my personal opinion, General Wickham was a fine officer and true gentleman, but his effectiveness as CFC commander was probably diminished as a result of 12/12.

To really understand the depth of American feelings on this matter, one must understand the code by which military officers live, embodied in the motto "duty, honor, and country." Central to this philosophy is that an officer will always tell another officer the truth. This rule is unbreakable. In battle, if an officer states his position falsely, he directly endangers the lives of his men and his comrades. Therefore, this unauthorized and unprofessional action by Chun Doo Hwan and his followers caused a rift that was difficult to heal for a long time. Americans felt that Chun and his followers had betrayed our trust. This would unfortunately dominate our bilateral military relationship in the crucial days ahead.

CHAPTER 7

Aftermath of 12/12

On the morning of December 13, 1979, I departed the Yongsan bunker, intending to return home. But I was intercepted on the way to my car by the Canadian attaché, Allan Klassen. Al was not at his best, having been out late the night before visiting Itaewon nightspots.[1] He had barely been to bed when he received a call from his ambassador, who wanted to know the details of what had transpired the night before. About this time he was also joined by the Philippine attaché, the Thai attaché, and several others, all with sleepy faces. Most of these officers were, in addition to their duties as military attachés, assigned to the United Nations command at Yongsan. Forces from their countries had participated in the Korean War, and these officers represented their countries at the periodic Panmunjom talks with the North Koreans. They asked me to brief them on the situation, for their governments were anxious to understand exactly what had happened.

Although we Americans by now had a feeling that the worst was over and that things for now were relatively calm, the rest of the international community in Seoul was just getting the news. The rumors that we had already dealt with, such as widespread fighting among South Korean forces and serious casualties, were beginning to fly around the foreign community. Some of these rumors were almost unbelievable. For example, one embassy had reported that Korea was at a state of near civil war and that the U.S. 2d Infantry Division had been ordered to Seoul to protect American and other foreign citizens. Many believed that an evacuation was imminent, and several individuals expressed concern for their own safety and that of their families. It was clear that the first order of business was to try and calm them down.

I explained the situation as we knew it, trying to convey a sense of calm and composure and emphasizing that there was no serious danger to the international community. What had happened was essentially an internal matter, I said, and the Korean authorities, to include Pres. Choi Kyu Ha and the legitimate government, were still in charge. This was only partially true, of course, but we did feel that there was only minimal danger and that the most important thing at this time was to avoid panic. There were several questions following my short briefing, and the group seemed satisfied and calmed when I left for my residence.

At home I had another briefing to perform. My wife had been awake all night, for the telephone had been ringing constantly. Most of the calls were from Korean friends, many of them military officers but also some civilians. The Japanese attaché had also called. My wife was calm but tired. Like everyone else she was eager to learn what had happened. I told her, and like a good army wife, she accepted the situation calmly and without much emotion, remarking dryly that she wished "they would conduct future coups during normal duty hours!" She then went to bed, and I began to return several of the calls, including the one from the Japanese attaché. He wanted to see me as soon as possible, and we agreed to meet at my residence later that morning.

A few minutes later the telephone rang once more. This time the call was from a Korean officer assigned to the 9th Division, commanded by Maj. Gen. Roh Tae Woo. This officer asked to see me on an urgent basis, and I immediately sensed that he was making the request under instruction. Since the 9th Division was one of those that had moved Combined Forces Command units without notification the night before, this was an opportunity to gain some additional insight into the situation, and I agreed to meet this officer the same day.

Another call was from the chief of the ROK Army Foreign Liaison Office (FLO). The purpose of this organization was to manage and control the activities of the foreign military attachés assigned to Korea. The FLO also was supposed to schedule events and keep us informed concerning military matters. In this case, however, the roles were reversed since it was the FLO seeking the information. Whether this was an attempt to determine how the U.S. Embassy was interpreting the 12/12 events or if the officer was truly confused and trying to determine what had happened for his own knowledge was uncertain. I suspect it was the latter since only a small group of the army had been involved in 12/12. The rest, like us, were trying to learn what had happened. Anyhow, I relayed the facts as we knew them and also told him he would probably be getting a new boss very soon. That was indeed the case—the following week his boss, the army chief of intelligence and a Class 8 member, was replaced. He retired soon afterward; the FLO gained a promotion.

A Visit from the Japanese Attaché

The Japanese military attaché, Col. Ahiro Hagino, arrived at my house in the late morning. Like myself, he still had not been to sleep and looked haggard and tired. I asked about the Japanese Embassy's assessment of the situation, which I learned was similar to our own. He then pulled from his pocket a notepad in which he had some handwritten notes listing the Korean military units that were suspected of having participated in the previous evening's activities. Although we were still in the process of compiling such information, our initial list was similar but not identical to his. Later it was determined that there were mistakes on both, but the Japanese had very accurate information, far better than any of the other attachés and their respective embassies.

I then mentioned to Hagino that I had seen him briefly the night before, walking rapidly from the DSC headquarters area toward his embassy. He looked surprised and said that he had been performing an inspection of the area but was stopped by a sentry and told to return to his embassy, which he did. We discussed some more matters, and then the colonel departed.

I was a little suspicious that the Japanese were able to be so well informed, thinking that they might have had some prior knowledge about 12/12. After considering all the facts, however, I dismissed the idea, though they might have been more culturally sensitive than we Americans to the earlier reports about Chun's possible reassignment and the pressure to remove Chung from the power structure of the army. Also, despite (or perhaps because of) their unpleasant history, the Japanese and Koreans share enough similarities in the way they think that they sometimes understand each other better than Americans are capable of doing. At any rate, their military attaché was well trained and hardworking, and that was probably the main reason they were so well informed.

A Visit from a 9th Division Officer

In the early afternoon I consulted with Colonel Blottie and some other members of the embassy staff. About midafternoon the officer from the 9th Division arrived. I had known him for several years (we remain good friends). He was a direct subordinate of Maj. Gen. Roh Tae Woo, and his mission was no secret to either them or us. He was here to determine how badly the previous night's events had damaged ROK-U.S. relations.

I gave him an honest and straightforward answer, that in the immediate and near term, it had damaged our countries' relations quite badly. Over the longer term, however, our common interests in the security of the Korean peninsula and in ensuring stability following 12/12 would dictate that we work together as harmoniously as possible. I was told that the portion of the 9th Division that moved into Seoul was the division's reserve regiment, not a unit that was on DMZ duty. This was, of course, an attempt to minimize the importance of what had happened in that regard. I replied that his distinction in our view did not excuse the illegal and unauthorized use of those forces that were diverted from their legitimate military duty and used for domestic political purposes. I also stated my opinion that any future such incident was unthinkable. He asked about General Wickham's reaction, and I told him that the general was very disappointed and could probably be expected to make his views known directly to the appropriate authorities in the very near future. We chatted a few more minutes before he departed to return to his headquarters. By now I had not slept in the last two days, so I took a warm shower and tried to sleep for a few hours.

Ambassador Gleysteen Meets with President Choi

By the morning of December 13, Ambassador William Gleysteen had been successful in his attempts to contact President Choi and had arranged a meeting that same day. After exchanging the usual pleasantries, Gleysteen stated to Choi that he wished to express the views of the U.S. government concerning the present situation. The ambassador then made two major points. First, he stressed the need for civilian control of the armed forces and pointed out the dangers of an independent military not responsible to a higher authority. Second, he expressed the U.S. government's strong support for the ongoing program of political liberalization. In this regard Gleysteen gave the longstanding U.S. view that only widespread and direct participation by the Korean people in the political process could ensure true stability of the ROK, that further interference by the military in this process could only have a negative effect. The meeting ended cordially, and the ambassador left, expressing his appreciation for having been granted the appointment on such short notice and hopeful that his words would encourage the desired results.[2]

In private, though, Ambassador Gleysteen was not optimistic. When he returned to the embassy, he drafted a message to Washington reporting the substance of the meeting in a straightforward manner. The tone of the report was very pessimistic and expressed serious doubt that the Choi government had either the will or the power to control the army.

In Washington the same day, Assistant Secretary of State Richard Holbrooke met with the ROK ambassador to convey a similar message. The American view of that meeting was that the Korean ambassador himself was either not yet fully mindful of the total implications of the 12/12 events or had received no instructions. Either way, he accepted the concerns expressed by Holbrooke without much comment and indicated that the conversation would be reported to Seoul.

Chun Doo Hwan Purges the Army

On December 14 sweeping changes were announced in the ROK Army hierarchy. Officers loyal to Chun were placed in key commands and staff positions, particularly in those units that were politically sensitive and might have the capability to launch an attempt at a countercoup. For example, 9th Division commander Major General Roh became commander of the Capital Defense Command, which included most of the combat forces in the Seoul area, and other classmates or trusted officers were placed in command of the Special Warfare Command, Third ROK Army, and several other units. In turn, these new commanders ensured that officers loyal to themselves were placed in command of subordinate regiments and battalions. Officers from Korean Military Academy Classes 11 and 12 moved ahead of their seniors in certain key staff positions as well. Widespread and wholesale retirements were ordered by the end of the month, especially among Class 8 officers. It was clear that the army was being purged and that Chun and his followers would now be in total effective control.

To my way of thinking, the events of December 14 were more significant than those of December 12 for at least three reasons. First was the consolidation of the army under Chun's control. Second and more importantly, these actions provided the first indication that Chun might have more on his mind than simply carrying out his investigatory responsibilities under martial law. After all, if his intention on 12/12 had been only to investigate President Park's assassination, why was it necessary to take complete control of the army? Third, it was confirming evidence, if indeed any was necessary by now, that the Choi government was incapable of exerting control over the new army leadership. Clearly Ambassador Gleysteen's meeting with President Choi had had no positive effect. From that point on it was obvious that civilian control of the military was a pipedream.

While the 12/12 incident led to the purge of the top army leadership, it also produced a sharp turn in the careers of numerous midlevel officers. One such person was my friend Col. Hwang Won Taek. Colonel Hwang was an extremely competent officer, having finished at or near the top of his class at the KMA. His prospects in the military were exceptionally bright until 12/12, for he had been promoted well ahead of his contemporaries on a regular basis. In fact, he had been selected as the senior assistant to General Chung and was serving in that capacity on 12/12. When Chung was arrested that night, Hwang was not present at the chief of staff's quarters but was in radio contact. When alerted that something serious was transpiring at the quarters, Hwang immediately returned, but his entry to the compound was blocked by forces loyal to Chun Doo Hwan (which, incidentally, were commanded by another good friend, Col. Kim Jin Young—see chapter 8). Hwang was unable to reach his boss, who was arrested and imprisoned but eventually released.

Following this incident, Colonel Hwang's career took a pronounced downward turn. Not trusted by the emerging powers in the army, and perhaps feared by Chun Doo Hwan and his supporters because of his popularity among the younger KMA classes, Hwang was assigned to an unimportant staff position at Second ROK Army headquarters in the southern area of Taegu, far from Seoul and any front-line command, a backwater for ambitious officers. His security clearance was also suspended, and he was in limbo for several years. Eventually Hwang was restored to a job working with the combined American-Korean forces but was passed over for troop command, the key to promotion in the Korean Army. His only offense had been loyalty to his boss.

With great frustration Colonel Hwang watched his less-talented peers pass him by for promotion, although he eventually attained the rank of brigadier general. Near his mandatory retirement date, he was selected for major general and served with distinction as the first Korean officer to head the Military Armistice Commission, the organization that negotiates and resolves military problems and issues with the North Koreans at Panmunjom.

This would be an interesting but not particularly significant story except that, following the election of Kim Young Sam to the presidency and Hwang's retirement from the army, he was "resurrected" and named ambassador to Panama. Although this was a relatively obscure posting, it was nonetheless a recognition of his talents and a tacit admission that his previous treatment had been wrong. Ambassador Hwang performed well and was soon given a more prestigious assignment, subsequently becoming an important player in the diplomatic hierarchy of South Korea. After the rise of Kim Dae Jung to the presidency, Hwang was appointed national security adviser to the president.

Gleysteen Meets with Chun Doo Hwan

Following Ambassador Gleysteen's unproductive meeting with President Choi on December 13, there was a division of opinion among the embassy staff as to whether it would be appropriate to meet with Chun Doo Hwan. The Political Section believed that it was inappropriate for the ambassador, who was the personal representative of the U.S. president, to meet with a major general on a coequal basis. As was often the case, the assessments and recommendations of Brewster's office and the Defense Attaché Office were somewhat different. I ascribe this primarily to the fact that diplomats sometimes seem to be more concerned with protocol and what is proper than with the reality of a situation. Intelligence officers and military men are more often action oriented, looking for information, and tend to approach a problem directly and with less concern for the subtleties of diplomacy. To us, Chun was a force to be reckoned with, and we saw no reason not to meet with him. Also, a direct meeting would lessen the chance that he would interpret our failure to show concern as acquiescence. General Wickham, who was still seething over the events of 12/12, argued against the meeting. At any rate, rather uncharacteristically, Ambassador Gleysteen ultimately decided to meet with Chun, although my recollection is that it was Chun who made the first suggestion of the meeting.[3] Regardless of who actually initiated it, the two men sat down together on December 14.

Gleysteen and Chun were very different types of people. The ambassador was soft-spoken, diplomatic, and tended to react unemotionally and analytically. He was a fine man but had a reputation of not being particularly forceful.[4] Chun, however, had spent most of his life in the army and was much more direct and forthright in his manner and demeanor. I had met him previously and considered him a strong personality, more than a match for Gleysteen.

At the meeting Ambassador Gleysteen made several points.[5] He expressed the U.S. government's deep concern over the events of 12/12. Much of his rhetoric was directed at the factionalism and disunity in the army, which invited North Korea to take advantage of the situation. Gleysteen's words in this regard were strong, but his quiet demeanor may have given the impression that he was not as angry as the words implied. He also stressed the importance of maintaining constitutional order and continuing the democratic reforms that would result in political liberalization.

Chun listened carefully and then addressed the ambassador's points one by one. The events of 12/12, he said, were accidental. He had never intended that the situation would become as complicated as it had, and the troop movements had not been preplanned but merely an outgrowth of his arrest of General Chung, which he saw as his duty. He expressed support of President Choi and the legitimate constitutional order, saying also that the division in the ROK Army was temporary and would be strengthened by the changes that were being made in the command structure that same day. He also denied any personal ambitions outside the army.

This meeting remained somewhat controversial even after it was finished. From the American perspective, we could now send a cable to Washington indicating that Chun had heard directly from the ambassador of our deep concerns and had been suitably warned and American concerns "put on the record." But I believe that in retrospect the meeting was more useful to Chun than to the United States. This was because Chun was now able to go back to his supporters and say that he had personally met with the U.S. ambassador and that his explanation of events had been understood and accepted. Of course it was true that his reasons had been understood, but they certainly were not accepted. Nonetheless, Chun used this meeting to suggest to his followers and others that the U.S. Embassy was now not opposed to his power move; perhaps he even implied that the United States supported him. In the days ahead, many Koreans approached me and other embassy staff asking if it were true that the U.S. government now supported Chun, and if not, why had Chun and Ambassador Gleysteen had such a "cozy" meeting? The fact that the meeting had taken place had unfortunately become more important than what was said at it, especially given the inability of the U.S. Embassy to get its message out to the public through the government-controlled Korean media.

Chun also requested a meeting with General Wickham, presumably to discuss and justify the 12/12 movements of CFC units and other issues. Serious debate occurred as to whether Wickham should agree to this. Most of his staff believed he should, but the embassy was opposed, arguing that the meeting should be refused in order to demonstrate U.S. anger over the 12/12 seizure of power. Ambassador Gleysteen personally requested that Wickham not meet with Chun. After some discussion, Wickham assented to the embassy's request.

I believe that this was a mistake, the first of several made in dealing with Chun and his followers during the period between 12/12 and the following May. I also believe that the embassy may have had some other reason for wanting to restrict Chun's access to Wickham. By now it was becoming evident that Chun held the real political power in Korea, and I think the embassy wanted to take the lead in dealing with him. Some rivalry had always existed between the U.S. military command at Yongsan and the embassy, and the diplomats did not want any "mixed signals" confusing the new Korean military leadership as to American policy objectives. Quite simply the embassy wanted to run the show.

Wickham did meet with other officials, however, including the prime minister, the new defense minister, and others. His message was consistent in these meetings—the unauthorized movement of ROK Army troops assigned to CFC OPCON must not happen again. He stressed that such incidents ran an unacceptable risk that CFC could not successfully defend against a North Korean attack. This point was reiterated in letters that were distributed to the appropriate authorities and in numerous discussions with senior Korean officers.

U.S. Policy Changes as a Result of 12/12

While these events were transpiring in Seoul, there were a series of meetings in Washington for the purpose of reviewing U.S. Korean policy in the aftermath of the military coup. As is normally the case in any full-scale policy review, almost all the appropriate departments of government were involved, but the major players were the White House, the State Department, and the Defense Department. Several meetings took place in the days following 12/12, and a number of options were considered, two of which were quite controversial.

The first option was to reduce, remove, or otherwise adjust U.S. military support for South Korea. Within this option were a variety of suboptions that ranged from withdrawal of some or all of the U.S. forces in Korea to canceling or postponing the annual security consultative meeting. The purpose of these actions would be to demonstrate American displeasure with the military takeover and force the new power structure to move toward a more democratic government or risk losing U.S. military support. In this regard, it should be recalled that some Carter government advisors had supported the withdrawal of U.S. forces from Korea earlier, and this faction saw the events of 12/12 as an opportunity to raise the troop-withdrawal issue again.

Fortunately the Defense Department strongly and forcefully opposed this course of action, arguing that such withdrawal was neither in the interest of South Korea nor the United States, for both had a strong requirement to maintain stability and peace on the Korean peninsula. For the same reason, a threat to engage in troop withdrawal would probably lack credibility with the new military leadership. Also, if carried out, force reduction would pose an unacceptable risk that might encourage North Korean provocations. Therefore, although it was briefly considered, troop withdrawal, either in full or in part, was discarded as a viable option.

More serious consideration was given to cancellation or postponement of the annual security consultative meeting. These bilateral gatherings were an important symbol of U.S. commitment to the ROK and could be canceled as a way of demonstrating disapproval without having the more serious effect that might result from an actual troop withdrawal. Accordingly, this option had more support.

Again, however, the Defense Department was strongly opposed to canceling or postponing the annual meeting. With lingering memories of the recent struggle over troop withdrawal, they made an aggressive argument that it was a mistake to link security policy with our political objectives to expand democracy in Korea. The Defense Department also argued that this critical period in South Korea demanded that we show solidarity in a military sense. Anything that detracted from that, even if it were primarily only a demonstration of disapproval rather than a concrete action, would be detrimental to our security interests both in Korea and East Asia. In the end, the security-consultative-meeting option was also rejected.

Economic sanctions were considered as well. But support for this alternative was weak across the board. The consensus of opinion was that sanctions would result in even more authoritarian policies. The ROK's economic situation was somewhat unsteady at the time.[6] It was felt that any actions that would make the situation worse would likely cause additional social unrest, more demonstrations, and ultimately result in an even more severe crackdown by the military. Further, sanctions were generally considered to be inappropriate between allies. Economic sanctions were discarded as an option.

Despite having ruled out three strong options, the consensus was that the U.S. government still needed to express its views forcefully and at the highest level. To this end, it was recommended that President Carter send a letter to President Choi that would express concern at the events of December 12 as strongly as possible. This communication was forwarded in early January, 1980, and expressed support for democratic reform and political reconciliation. The letter stated that Carter was "deeply distressed" by the events of 12/12 and warned that similar occurrences in the future "would have serious consequences for our close cooperation."[7] The U.S. Embassy attempted to distribute this letter as widely as possible so that the American position would be well known by ordinary Koreans, but as a practical matter, it did not seem to have any important effect.

As a result of the Washington meetings, it was becoming clear that the United States had very limited options to influence the situation. Finally, a three-legged policy was adopted that would guide our actions over the next several months. These "marching orders" were as follows:

- Attempt to preserve momentum toward a broadly based democratic government under civilian leadership.
- Continue to deter North Korean aggression.
- Strive to keep the new ROK military leadership focused on its primary role of defending the country against attack.

As a practical matter, this was really not much of a change in U.S. policy prior to 12/12. It did have a new urgency, however, and the embassy and Washington were united in trying to carry it out in the days ahead. Unfortunately we were only partially successful.

The "Gag Order" and Censorship

By late December, 1979, things had settled down to some extent. The embassy focused its efforts toward reestablishing the progress toward democracy, and USFK attempted to put the events of 12/12 behind it and stay focused on its military mission. General Wickham had been subject to some criticism in Washington for having "lost control" of the ROK Army, and he therefore spent a great deal of time visiting front-line units and emphasizing training and readiness. American military officers were instructed not to discuss the 12/12 events with their Korean counterparts and to avoid political discussions. These orders were well designed to demonstrate the nonpolitical nature of the military and set the example of a professional officer corps. The negative side of such an order was to establish a general feeling that all was now well and it was once again "business as usual."

There was another downside to this "gag order." Many ROK officers had very little information about how the outside world was viewing events in Korea. Their own access to accurate information was restricted, just as with most ordinary Korean citizens. On numerous occasions various Korean officers would approach their American counterparts seeking copies of magazines such as *Newsweek* or *Time* or similar international news sources. In some of these cases, the information was for their superior officers, many of whom were also desperately seeking information. The true situation at the time was that some of these men were opposed to Chun Doo Hwan and his group, and others might have been if they had known the full story. For this reason, the ruling group carefully controlled the news media during this period.

The embassy was well aware of this pervasive censorship and was increasingly concerned that the position of the U.S. government was not widely understood among Koreans. At one time it was proposed that we might go directly to the Korean people, perhaps by using leaflet distribution or similar methods. Unlike in 1987, when U.S. officials in the ROK would again face an internal political crisis, such activities were not approved, for they were considered incompatible with our diplomatic function.[8] The ultimate result of this communications failure was that again we were widely perceived as supporting the Chun group. Had we taken more aggressive action to get our message directly to the Korean people, this might not have been the case.

The First Countercoup Plot

Early in 1980, rumors began circulating concerning the possibility of opposition to Chun and his group within the ROK Army. At first these were not taken seriously, but such reports continued for several days, and we eventually became concerned.

On a cold January night, I met with an officer who had been close to Chung Sung Wha and also had many strong contacts among the Class 8 group, which had been ousted from the army by subordinate officers from Classes 11 and 12. This meeting took place in a tearoom near Samgakji, not far from the Ministry of National Defense and ROK Army Headquarters. I asked this officer if he had also heard these rumors. The answer was startling.

This individual, in whom I placed much confidence, said that not only were the rumors true but there was even an organized group actively considering a countercoup against Chun and his followers. He claimed to be in close contact with this group and asked what would be the U.S. Embassy's view of such a countercoup. I realized that such matters were far outside the authority of an officer of my rank and position. Although I had no desire to continue such a conversation, I did stress that any conflict between ROK Army elements would be a disaster both for South Korea and the United States.

I reported this conversation to Colonel Blottie and Bob Brewster the next day. Brewster did not seem overly surprised. He said that he had heard similar stories and that I should continue to stay alert to such reports. He was also quite clear that embassy policy was to discourage any such attempt at a countercoup.

A few weeks later I heard from a reliable source within the embassy that there had indeed been such a plot and that at least one member of the embassy's senior staff had been approached and asked point blank if the U.S. government would support such an attempt. I believe that the one approached was Brewster but have no direct knowledge of that.[9]

For numerous reasons, the U.S. government actively and strongly opposed a countercoup. First, to do otherwise would have been against our existing policy, which was to keep the ROK military focused on its external security mission and out of extralegal, politically oriented activities. Second, support of a countercoup would have been far outside accepted diplomatic parameters. For an embassy that would not even consider the use of leaflets to disseminate its government's position directly to the Korean people, involvement in a countercoup was unthinkable. Further, the Carter administration would never have approved it, despite its dislike for Chun and suspicions of his motives.

Besides these legal and policy considerations, there were other factors. Chun and his followers were in effective control of the army units that would be most important in a coup attempt; therefore the attempt would likely fail. They also appeared to have the support of younger officers, especially some from Class 17 and below who were at the time commanding the regiments and battalions whose loyalty would be necessary to successfully carry out a seizure of government. There also were indications on the political front that the government would honor previous commitments to political reform; at this time the embassy and Washington were still hopeful that democracy would prevail. The last thing the U.S. government wanted under these circumstances was another coup—we were still recovering from the first one. For these reasons, we actively and aggressively discouraged this plot. Some may say this was an error or suggest it proves that we secretly supported Chun, but I think the reasons given above are sensible and that we reacted properly in light of the situation at the time.

CHAPTER 8

Prelude to Kwangju

By early 1980 things had begun to settle down to the extent that we could do some rational thinking about what actions, if any, the United States could take to promote democracy and reduce the chances of a full military takeover. Most of us realized that, whatever actions the United States might take, they probably would not be the decisive factor. The real outcome of the struggle for democracy would ultimately have to come from the Koreans themselves and how they resolved the various competing political power centers. Although our official policy was to encourage the transition to a freely elected government, in reality most knowledgeable observers feared that the trend was away from democracy and toward continued military rule. My own analysis was that there was still a chance for a transition to democracy throughout the late winter and early spring of 1980 and that it certainly was not inevitable that a new power structure in the ROK Army necessarily precluded democratization.

This assessment was reached primarily because I had firsthand experience with many of the Class 11 and younger groups, particularly Class 17, and was familiar with their thinking. Quite frankly there was a lot of truth in their claim to be better educated, better trained, and probably better equipped to lead the army than their predecessors. They more easily commanded the loyalty of their subordinates and generally were more widely respected than the previous leadership. Also, although some corruption was still prevalent in the army, in 1979–80 the younger officers who supported Chun Doo Hwan and his followers were generally considered to be less corrupt and more professional than their seniors. Like most military men, however, they greatly valued stability and order.

One such officer with whom I became well acquainted in those days was Col. Kim Jin Young, who was the de facto leader of Class 17, was very close to Chun Doo Hwan (both were from the Taegu area), and had played a critical role in the events of 12/12. At this time Kim was commanding an important regiment in the Seoul area, and I visited his unit from time to time.

Once I gave a briefing to his staff officers regarding China, where I had traveled the year before. In those days China was still a closed country for the most part, so this briefing was in great demand. At any rate, we became good friends, and I must confess that he made a very favorable impression. He exuded self-confidence and walked with a sort of permanent swagger. Later he was promoted to full general and eventually became chief of staff of the army before being abruptly removed by Pres. Kim Young Sam. I would see him again often in the years to follow.

Official U.S. Contacts with Chun Doo Hwan

Just as Colonel Kim influenced my own thinking, Major General Chun himself was quite skillful at convincing the U.S. Embassy that democracy was still possible. By late January, 1980, Bob Brewster had established direct contact with him. I am not certain how often or how regularly they met, but it was often enough for Brewster to form some opinions as to future developments. I believe these opinions were generally optimistic.

Indeed, there was reason for optimism. Despite earlier fears, the constitutional order had been preserved. In addition, some political prisoners had been released and media censorship, while still prevalent, was not exercised with the same iron hand that it had been earlier. Controls were relaxed as well on political activities on college campuses. In February dissident Kim Dae Jung was allowed to participate in the political process once again. This was particularly significant, for he had a large following in the United States; the relaxation of restrictions on his activities resulted in some favorable press reports in Washington.[1] The combined effect of these events was enough that embassy reporting during this period continued to have a positive tone.[2]

In mid-February Gen. John Wickham met with Major General Chun.[3] This was the first meeting between the two since 12/12. I am not certain why General Wickham changed his mind about talking with Chun, but I believe that this time the idea for such a meeting came from the American side.[4] There was a feeling at United States Forces Korea Headquarters that, since the embassy was now meeting with Chun on a fairly regular basis, it no longer served any useful purpose for Wickham not to meet with him. Also, Wickham was still under criticism in Washington for not having taken a strong enough posture with the younger ROK Army generals after 12/12—this may also have been a motivation.

At this meeting General Wickham emphasized the same points that had previously been made by Ambassador Gleysteen and others such as Brewster. These included the importance of civilian control of the military, progress toward democratization, and adherence to Central Forces Command OPCON procedures. By now, however, more than two months had passed since 12/12, and Chun was in a much stronger position.

The American and Korean sides had somewhat different accounts of this meeting. The Americans felt that it had been generally satisfactory, although Wickham reported later to Washington that he was not certain that he had made any positive impression on Chun. The Korean version of the meeting was that it was dominated by Chun, who despite his status as the junior officer, lectured Wickham about the realities of the Korean peninsula, dismissed his concerns somewhat abruptly, and was condescending and almost arrogant in his manner. I was not personally present, but from discussing the meeting with others, I tend to believe that the Korean version is more accurate. At any rate, the talk was hardly a success from any perspective and probably only served to make worse the personal relationship between the two men, which was not good to begin with.

I have never believed that USFK handled its overall relations with the ROK Army very skillfully during this period. Its intentions were good, but even two months after 12/12, American officers continued to pound away on the OPCON issue at every opportunity. By now, even the officers who were anti-Chun had heard enough about OPCON. Also, the order not to discuss political matters with Korean officers had been taken to extremes. This had been expanded in practice to preclude even talking with members of the U.S. Embassy concerning what ROK officers might be thinking or rumors that a U.S. officer might have heard. The net effect of this was to reduce the U.S. government's level of understanding about what the rank-and-file Korean military officers were thinking. Thus, our appreciation for the overall ROK military point of view tended to be framed by what Chun was telling Brewster or by what I was learning from my contacts, many of whom were Chun supporters. Unfortunately we missed the opportunity to get a broader perspective from wider sources. This probably would not have made any difference in later events, but we might have used a broader sample of opinion to find ways to reduce Chun's support in the army, which might have influenced him to take more moderate actions when the political situation deteriorated in late April and May.

The bad personal relationship between Generals Wickham and Chun was also unfortunate. Obviously it would have been difficult for the two men, who had far different personalities, to have been close friends. But both had an obligation to the security of South Korea and should have been able to put their personal differences aside to work for the common good. Neither did, and the relationship remained bad and even grew worse. Perhaps if Wickham had accepted the first meeting in December, 1979, the two could have worked more closely together, and Wickham might have had more influence on Chun's actions. But by February it was too late.

This relationship grew worse after an incident on the Yongsan Golf Course in early spring. Chun, by now a three-star general, had arrived at Yongsan for lunch and a round of golf. In those days, since he was concerned about his own safety, Chun traveled with an impressive number of bodyguards. When the minister of defense, the Joint Chiefs of Staff chairman, or other senior Korean officers used this facility, they arrived with a single aide and driver. Chun, in contrast, had an entourage fit for a king. At one point he had a security detail and personal staff of almost twenty people, and several cars were necessary to transport them all. General Wickham either saw or was told of the size of this group and apparently was upset by the ostentatious display. He directed that Chun's large detail not be allowed to use the clubhouse and other facilities until such time as they were reduced to a level consistent with other officers of his rank and position. Wickham made it clear that Chun himself was welcome, though with a reduced staff. This was a reasonable request, but either through misunderstanding or an unwillingness to comply, Chun was infuriated. He and his group left in a big huff, never to return. The feelings between Wickham and Chun had reached a new low point.

Chun Becomes KCIA Director

In March and early April, 1980, the South Korean economic picture began to deteriorate. There were violent strikes involving miners along the east coast, and we began to receive reports that indicated the military might be having second thoughts about the liberal direction of the political process. The relaxation on political activity had resulted in some inflammatory talk from the opposition, and the military began to warn of "instability." Korea was still under martial law, though at a reduced level. Control of the media had lessened, but some censorship still existed. The embassy had urged the Korean government to lift martial law and establish a timetable for direct elections, but without success. Finally, student protests continued, particularly over martial law, even though these were mainly confined to campuses and were generally nonviolent.[5]

With Chun in control of the military and the government of Choi Kyu Ha weak and ineffective, only the Korean Central Intelligence Agency (KCIA) remained as a potential power center. The KCIA was already weakened at the top by the actions of its former director, Kim Jae Kyu, the assassin of President Park. Now Chun moved to take control of the organization before it could reinvigorate itself.

On April 14 Chun was appointed KCIA director. The announcement came late in the afternoon, a mere half hour after the U.S. Embassy was informed of the move. Although some of us had speculated that Chun might try to do such a thing, we had thought that he would do it indirectly by having a surrogate appointed, not himself personally. This meant that he now controlled both the military and the civilian intelligence agencies. Soon after his appointment, Chun began purging many positions at the KCIA in the same manner he had done in the army during the days following 12/12.

Now it was clear that Chun's ambitions had expanded. The prevailing feeling in Washington was that it would be necessary for the U.S. government to take positive action in order to oppose this move. There were meetings held similar to those following 12/12, but again there appeared to be few courses of action available that would have the desired effect of retarding Chun's march to power while not hurting the overall interest of the U.S. government and the Korean people. Ultimately it was decided that it was necessary to demonstrate that failure to implement political reform, and further attempts to consolidate power by Chun would have a negative effect on U.S.-ROK relations. Accordingly the U.S. government informed ROK officials that the security consultative meeting was indefinitely postponed, hoping this would deter Chun.[6]

Many of us disagreed with the meeting's postponement. The Defense Department, which had opposed linking our political objectives in South Korea to security policy, had argued strongly against this option. Although they were unsuccessful, their objections did result in having the meeting "postponed" rather than "canceled." This had the effect of watering down the desired message. Also, it gave the correct impression that the U.S. government was not united in its desire to punish Chun. This was reinforced because virtually none of the U.S. military in Korea supported the decision to postpone the security consultative meeting, which became well known to the ROK military within a few days.[7] Thus, the move by Washington was totally ineffective; indeed, it served to make Chun stronger. It also tended to split the embassy and USFK, since USFK blamed the State Department and by extension the embassy for supporting the postponement.

By early May, 1980, demonstrations had grown both in number of participants and frequency. There were reports that the police might not be able
to handle these protests by themselves and that consideration was being
given to using military forces in a back-up role. The U.S. government was
especially concerned with these reports and instructed Ambassador
Gleysteen to convey American concerns to the Korean authorities. By now,
although we still dealt formally with the Choi government, the embassy
decided to deal directly with Chun as well since he was the actual power.
This was a measure of Chun's success to this point, and even the embassy
Political Section did not object. In response to his instructions, therefore,
Gleysteen arranged another meeting with Chun, this time for May 9.[8]

From the American perspective, this meeting went much better than the
one in December, 1979.[9] Gleysteen had been receiving regular reports from
Bob Brewster concerning his contacts with Chun, and some of Brewster's
optimism may have rubbed off on the ambassador. Chun listened closely to
the ambassador's concerns and replied in a confident and measured tone.
He said that the situation was serious but certainly not critical. Military force
would be used only as a last resort, he said, and expressed his personal opinion that it would not be necessary at all. Chun blamed the unrest on a small
number of radical elements and seemed to imply that he intended to treat
the expected demonstrations with moderation. His body language and demeanor in no way suggested that a crisis was at hand.

Gleysteen then expressed the well-known American views that only by
allowing the people to participate in their own government could South
Korea enjoy true stability and that the key to quieting potential unrest was
to convince the demonstrators that progress was being made toward that
goal. He asked that a timetable for democracy be established and adhered
to. He also urged Chun not to crack down on opposition politicians, stress-
ing that it was one thing to take action against a small number of true radicals but quite another to risk alienating the many moderate students who
formed the majority of the demonstrators. Finally, Gleysteen cautioned
against taking any actions that would cause the general populace to join
the crowds.

In contrast to their previous meeting, this one ended fairly cordially. Following Chun's departure, Gleysteen reported to Washington that he now believed that the situation was under control and that there was a good chance
that the upcoming demonstrations would be dealt with in a moderate

manner. At the end of the day, the ambassador was reasonably upbeat, but I think this was a misunderstanding of the Korean side's intention.

That same day General Wickham met with the ROK defense minister and JCS chairman.[10] He pointed out the danger of using military forces against civilians, but he also stressed the importance of coordination with CFC in the event troops were so used. Combining these two subjects together was a mistake, for it seemed to indicate to the Koreans that Wickham might be already resigned to the use of troops. Thus, his earlier advice against using military forces to control civilians lost much of its power.

My Meeting with Roh Tae Woo

The same day that Gleysteen was meeting with Chun, I was finishing some routine administrative work when I received a telephone call from the ROK Army chief of foreign liaison, Col. Lee Sang Hun. He asked if I were available to meet with Gen. Roh Tae Woo that afternoon. I replied that I was. He then said that a car would pick me up in ten minutes in front of the U.S. Embassy. I promptly finished what I was doing and left my office.

The car arrived almost immediately. We drove to General Roh's headquarters in a compound just behind the famous Korea House restaurant, where many foreigners often gathered to enjoy typical Korean food and some cultural entertainment. As I entered the area, I observed that the soldiers were very active, were busy checking their vehicles, and had their combat gear close by. This was not their normal defense posture, and although they did not appear to be on full alert, they were certainly at an alert status higher than normal. My assessment was that they could be deployed in a very short time if the order was given.

I was met at the front of the headquarters of the Capital Defense Command by Colonel Lee and escorted up the stairs to the waiting room where the commanding general met his visitors. Within a few moments, Roh Tae Woo entered. A pleasant, outgoing man, he was dressed in his neatly pressed combat-fatigue uniform, with highly shined boots, presenting an impressive and distinguished appearance. He greeted me warmly, and we made small talk while the customary *InSam Cha* was served.[11] Soon the general turned to more serious matters.

He began on a philosophical note, reflecting on his days at the KMA, noting that it was founded by an American general, James Van Fleet, and that to a large degree the education received there reflected American values. He spoke of the writings of Thomas Jefferson and described democracy as an ideal form of government. He mentioned the long friendship and close relationship between the Korean and American people, and the importance of maintaining those close ties in the future. Despite these close ties and the many similarities between us, however, there were also differences. The United States, for example, enjoyed secure borders, with Canada to the north and Mexico to the south. This situation was quite different in South Korea, with a hostile and well-armed, fully deployed enemy force only a few miles from Seoul. Because of this important difference, he explained, Korea could not afford the type of continuing internal friction and political fragmentation that might be acceptable in other countries. It would be irresponsible to allow the country to become unstable in the name of political freedom, especially if that freedom invited the North to exploit the situation. No responsible officer could allow such a thing to happen if he had the means to prevent it.

Roh then made an analogy. "Suppose," he said, "you are holding in your hands a large number of diamonds. Some of these diamonds are real, but some are not, they are only glass. How do you tell the difference? Only an expert can know immediately, but with time and practice one can learn enough to recognize the true diamonds. Do not be fooled by false diamonds," he warned. The point of this analogy was that, given time, the U.S. government would be able to recognize and presumably appreciate the real leaders in Korea. I understood this to be a reference to the Class 11 and younger group that he represented, who were the "true diamonds." I assumed the "false diamonds" were either the former army leaders or perhaps opposition politicians such as Kim Dae Jung, although Roh did not specify.

This meeting lasted more than an hour. The impression I had upon departure was of a composed and rational officer who was not unreasonable but was strongly committed to maintaining stability. He certainly would not let the internal situation deteriorate past the present situation. Also, the apparent increased alert status indicated to me that some sort of use of military forces was probable in the near future.

Returning to the embassy, I drafted a report to my Washington headquarters summarizing Roh's remarks and adding my personal observations concerning the increased alert status. I also stated unequivocally that, in my professional judgment, the military was fully prepared to use all resources at its command to maintain domestic stability, including active army forces. By the time I finished, it was well after duty hours. Had I waited for embassy clearance, the report would have had to be coordinated with the Political Section, which probably would have delayed its transmission. I believed that

Washington needed the information and analysis immediately, so I sent it on my own authority.

The report was read with great interest both within the embassy and in Washington. Colonel Blottie scheduled a meeting with General Roh as a result of my report, apparently in order to form his own opinion. My report was somewhat controversial, possibly because the ambassador had sent a rather more optimistic assessment to Washington following his meeting with Chun. Blottie's feeling after his meeting with Roh was similar to my own—the situation was reaching a critical point, and the military would not let it go much further without stepping in. Thus, by the middle of May, there was some division of opinion on the American side concerning the likelihood of the use of military force. The embassy, particularly the Political Section, considered it less likely; the military attachés, more likely.

Why did General Roh ask to meet with me, an official somewhat down the hierarchy in the embassy? My Korean-language skills were undoubtedly part of the explanation. Further, I had a good reputation with the Koreans as a hardworking attaché who understood their country's situation better than most. Also, Colonel Lee or Col. Kim Jin Young, who was extremely close to Rho, may have recommended me as a reliable and useful channel.

Wickham Meets with Chun Again

On May 13 Generals Wickham and Chun met again.[12] Chun now blamed the student demonstrations and general unrest on North Korean clandestine activities. Exactly what these activities were was never specified. He implied that the situation was very serious and that North Korea might very well be preparing to attack at any time.

Since the U.S. side had access to the most accurate intelligence information on North Korea, and General Wickham was briefed on that situation almost every morning, he directly challenged Chun's statement. There were no signs that an attack was imminent, Wickham responded. He then stated the U.S. position that continued progress toward democracy and political liberalization was the best means of deterring North Korea and ensuring stability in the ROK. The meeting ended without either side making much of an impression on the other's point of view.

Indeed, by this time the relationship between Chun and Wickham had deteriorated to a point where neither man had much influence on the other. Wickham's report of this latest meeting centered on Chun's pessimistic assessment of the domestic situation and his fixation on a North Korean threat. For the first time, Wickham stated his frank opinion that Chun intended to use these arguments as a pretext to take those steps that would allow him to move directly into the Blue House. This assessment further increased the distance between the U.S. Embassy, which was still hopeful that constitutional processes would prevail, and the U.S. military, which supported General Wickham's view.

Rumors of North Korean Activities

ROK authorities quickly spread around Seoul rumors of North Korean activities. This had become such a hot topic that the State Department issued a statement to the press on May 13 designed to counter them. "From our information we see no movement of troops in North Korea out of the usual and we see no movement which would lead us to believe that some sort of attack upon the South is imminent."[13]

In Seoul that same day I spent several hours at the intelligence center in the Yongsan bunker, personally monitoring the North Korean forces, and was unable to determine anything out of the ordinary. By now it was clear that the stories about North Korea were being cooked up in order to justify further domestic crackdowns and related activities.

Contacts with Opposition Leaders

Ambassador Gleysteen became even more actively involved at trying to head off a confrontation between the military and opposition elements.[14] On May 14 he met with the Blue House secretary general in order to urge restraint and moderation in dealing with opposition politicians and student demonstrators. General Wickham had left for the United States the previous evening, but his deputy delivered a similar message to the ROK minister of defense.

Gleysteen also contacted opposition leaders such as Kim Young Sam, Kim Dae Jung, and others to ask that they exercise restraint as well and urge moderation by their followers. By now, however, antigovernment protests had reached such a point that it was uncertain whether the opposition leadership could even control its own followers. The leaders did cooperate to some extent, but these efforts were not very successful since the government-controlled media failed to give their calls for moderation adequate publicity. The size of the demonstrations had by now grown to quite large proportions but had not yet turned violent.

Indeed, for a period of time on May 15–16, it appeared that reason might prevail. There were no demonstrations of significance in Seoul on May 16, and a hopeful feeling grew that perhaps the crisis had passed. The National Assembly was scheduled to meet on May 20, and speculation was high that it would call on the government to enact the necessary reforms and lift martial law. President Choi, who was on an official visit to the Middle East, cut short his trip and returned to Seoul on May 17 because of the growing crisis. There was hope that this meant some sort of reconciliation was on the horizon. Unfortunately just the opposite was about to happen.

CHAPTER 9

Kwangju and Its Aftermath

The first hard evidence that the authorities would return to full martial law rather than a negotiated settlement occurred on May 16, 1980, when Korean military authorities notified Combined Forces Command of their intent to withdraw elements of the 20th Division from CFC OPCON.[1] This later became quite a controversial issue (which I will discuss shortly), but at the time it was treated rather routinely. In response, CFC authorities acknowledged the notification but requested that alternative forces be assigned. While this was being discussed, events elsewhere began to move very rapidly.[2]

Concerned at the apparent turn of events from reconciliation to the hard-line stance favored by Chun Doo Hwan, Ambassador Gleysteen once more visited the Blue House on May 17.[3] We had heard rumors that Kim Dae Jung or other dissident leaders might be arrested, and Gleysteen warned Blue House Secretary General Choi Kwang Soo that any such action would likely lead to increased violence. By now, of course, the decision to declare complete martial law had been made by the military, and Pres. Choi Kyu Ha's recall was only for the purpose of having him rubber-stamp the decision. That same evening the U.S. Embassy was officially notified that full martial law would be reimposed throughout South Korea beginning at midnight.[4] About the same time, we began to receive reports of the arrests of some student leaders and opposition politicians, including Kim Dae Jung, Kim Young Sam, Kim Jong Pil, and others. Soon thereafter the National Assembly was closed at bayonet point. It appeared that this martial law would be even more harsh than previous versions.

Ambassador Gleysteen was dismayed.[5] He was instructed by Washington to deliver a sharp protest to the Blue House, which he did on the eighteenth, the first day of martial law. He met with President Choi, who by now had returned to Seoul and had formally authorized these actions. Choi justified himself by saying that the alternative was to totally lose control of the government because of the inability to contain the demonstrations. Gleysteen responded by calling for the immediate release of the opposition politicians, but by now he was merely following instructions; the ambassador had no realistic hope that Choi would respond favorably.[6]

That same day Bob Brewster met with Chun Doo Hwan to deliver the same strong protest. Chun replied that "impure elements" and "radicals" had taken control of the demonstrations and that the government had been forced to act as a result. Brewster was especially disappointed by this response, for he had been led to believe by Chun in their earlier contacts that such hard-line actions would be taken only in the most extreme emergency. I frankly think Brewster was embarrassed by this turn of events, and at this point he completely lost confidence in Chun's willingness to tell him the truth. Their relationship had been reasonably good to this point. In fact, Brewster was probably the only U.S. government official who had such a relationship with Chun since 12/12—now that was gone.[7]

There was at least one positive result of the May declaration of martial law. From the eighteenth forward, there was no longer any difference of opinion between the embassy and the U.S. military as to Chun's intentions. Following the report by Brewster of his meeting, and having assimilated the widespread reports of the extent of the crackdown, Ambassador Gleysteen now gave Washington his assessment of the situation: that Chun Doo Hwan and the military had all but formally taken over the country.[8]

A Slow Response

Following the imposition of total martial law, we in the embassy were initially caught up in trying to understand the depth and implications of what had happened. The mood in Seoul was sullen and defiant, but there was no violent opposition. South Korea had experienced martial law on several previous occasions, and it had never resulted in widespread violence; just the opposite was normally the case. Also, there was a widespread American mindset that believed that the ROK military, despite its disciplined training and reputation as a tough and effective fighting force, would never fire its weapons on its own people. Former president Syngman Rhee had been forced out of office when such a thing happened in April, 1960, and it was almost impossible for us to believe that it could happen again, especially in 1980.

On Monday, May 19, the embassy was contacted by David Miller, the director of the U.S. Information Services Center in Kwangju, who relayed reports told to him by local citizens that widespread rioting had taken place. He said that there had been some serious casualties and that ROK Army special warfare troops were being blamed. The same morning U.S. Forces Korea received a similar call from the U.S. Air Force base at Kwangju. Later in the day other reports began to trickle in that indicated that the situation in Kwangju was quite different from Seoul.[9]

By midday on Tuesday, May 20, rumors were flying thickly. The embassy and USFK had made inquiries of the Korean military authorities but were unable to get any reliable information as to the true situation. In the afternoon I dropped by unannounced at the office of a Korean Army lieutenant colonel who was a native of Kwangju and had formerly been on the staff of Chun Doo Hwan. This officer took me aside, and we walked outside together to the parking lot, where he told me what was happening in Kwangju. Earlier he had called his home there and had received a firsthand report from his parents. They had said the situation was terrible and that the special warfare soldiers had lost control. His parents had seen several bodies, including one almost on their own doorstep. He told me that the Ministry of National Defense and official ROK military sources were concealing this information from U.S. officials and were downplaying the extent of the problem. He also said there were other riots and violence in the cities of Mokpo and Naju. I had known this officer well for several years and believed him to be trustworthy and truthful. His close association with Chun meant that he was taking a big chance in giving me this information. "Please have your government get this stopped," he pleaded. I promised I would do my best and immediately drove back to the embassy.

Even by late on the twentieth, we were unsure of the extent of the tragedy in Kwangju.[10] Despite my report, which was given directly to Col. Don Blottie and Bob Brewster as soon as I returned, there was some disbelief that things could really be that bad. It was the next day before the true dimensions of what had happened were fully accepted.[11] By then, of course, it was already too late to influence the situation.

On the morning of May 21, I proposed to Colonel Blottie that I go personally to Kwangju to assess the situation and see what we could do to help. We had arranged for a U.S. military aircraft to fly me into the U.S. air base, and from there I would try to enter the city, which was blocked off by ROK Army forces. This mission was given some consideration but eventually disapproved by Gleysteen, who was concerned about the danger. To me, it was just part of being a soldier and certainly no more dangerous than what I had experienced previously in Vietnam, but I respected the ambassador's wishes.[12] Soon thereafter the embassy ordered a total evacuation of all American citizens from Kwangju.

Activities in Washington

Washington was slow to respond to events in Kwangju. Part of the problem was that the embassy was late to react and report on events there, but the U.S. foreign-policy apparatus was also preoccupied with events in Iran, where the holding of American hostages had led recently to an unsuccessful rescue mission, the resignation as secretary of state of Cyrus Vance, and his replacement by Edmund Muskie.[13] It was not until May 22 that a crisis team met and an official statement was issued. Muskie chaired the crisis meeting, and the results were an updated policy statement as follows:

• Advise the Korean government to restore order in Kwangju through dialogue and minimum use of force in order to avoid sowing the seeds of wide disorder.
• After resolution of the problem in Kwangju, continue pressure for responsive political structures and broadly based civilian government.
• Continue signals that the U.S. will defend South Korea from North Korean attack.[14]

These were our new "marching orders," and both Ambassador Gleysteen and Gen. John Wickham, who had now returned to Seoul from a trip stateside, moved quickly to carry them out. General Wickham met with the ROK military authorities several times and urged that any military steps taken to reestablish order be carried out with minimum force necessary to accomplish the mission.[15] USFK also dispatched AWACS early warning aircraft and naval units to Korea. Ambassador Gleysteen urged civilian officials to use restraint and suggested that ROK government leaders apologize for the excessive use of force.[16] Since such an act would be a direct admission that they were responsible for the deaths at Kwangju, however, such an apology was never seriously considered.

Because of the slow response to the terrible events in Kwangju, none of the actions taken by the U.S. government saved any lives. Most of our activities now were designed to assist the Korean government in its efforts to reestablish order without further bloodshed.

Most of the civilian casualties at Kwangju occurred at the hands of the Special Warfare Command troops in the first day or two following full martial law. By direction of the ROK government, these units had never been under CFC control. Although these troops were highly trained for the behind-the-lines operations directed at North Korea and, therefore, should logically have been under CFC authority, the Korean leaders had consistently resisted such suggestions. Quite frankly these forces were considered by most serious Korea-watchers to be earmarked for political-type activities such as anticoup protection. Also, they were often among the first units called out during martial law. The special-warfare commander was always personally approved by the president as were the heads of the Defense Security Command and Capital Defense Command. In 1980 these commanders were all close associates of Chun Doo Hwan.

The 20th Division was a different story. This was a CFC division, although some of its elements had been removed from CFC control during 12/12. It now appeared that Korean authorities intended to use this division to restore order in Kwangju. Because of General Wickham's constant and continuing protests over the unauthorized movement of CFC forces during 12/12, the ROK military was now extremely careful to consult with the U.S. side regarding the use of the 20th Division. This presented the Americans with a real dilemma.

The 20th Division was one of the few units trained in riot-control procedures, which in theory meant that its utilization in Kwangju would result in fewer civilian casualties. Since minimum loss of life was our objective, this was a very important consideration. Certainly the 20th's use would be preferable to the special-warfare units; even the Korean military had no desire to use these forces again.

In later official statements on this, the U.S. government maintained that it had no power to refuse the use of the 20th Division because, under the terms of the CFC charter, either country could withdraw its own forces upon notification—no approval was necessary or required.[17] This is technically and legally true, but in this case my recollection is that we participated very much in the decision process.

Indeed, I believe that it was the preplanned intention of Chun and his followers to involve the United States as much as possible in the events in Kwangju. As a result, the same Korean military authorities who a day or two before were concealing information from us now were eager to share every detail concerning the 20th Division's movements and operational plans. They went so far as to directly ask the U.S. leaders if they objected to use of the 20th. After consultations with Washington, both General Wickham and Ambassador Gleysteen agreed to its deployment.

I do not mean to imply in any way that the American side "ordered" or "approved" this decision, but it has always seemed to me that, in later attempts to explain this issue, we tried to hide behind technical and legal provisions of the CFC charter, when ethically and morally we were obligated to explain this situation more frankly to the Korean people. The fact was that we were consulted in great detail on this issue and reached the same decision, although perhaps more reluctantly, than ROK authorities.

Attempts at Negotiation

Despite the movement of the 20th Division to Kwangju and its ongoing preparation to retake the city, the U.S. Embassy was still actively trying to facilitate a negotiated settlement. An informal citizen's committee comprised of local leaders had been formed in that town, and Ambassador Gleysteen was trying to arrange a meeting between this group and martial-law authorities.[18] The embassy's Political Section believed that such an approach might succeed; indeed, the citizen's committee appeared to have been able to calm the city to some extent. It appeared at one point that such a meeting was possible, but this apparently fell through at the last moment over procedural details.

In another effort to defuse the situation and also to ensure that American views reached the people of Kwangju, a series of leaflets were prepared. These fliers appealed for calm and restraint, urging a negotiated settlement to the crisis. The original plan had been to drop these leaflets over Kwangju by U.S. military helicopters; however, martial-law authorities objected at the last minute, citing airspace control and safety problems. Instead, they offered to drop the leaflets using ROK military aircraft. They never carried out this promise and actually actively helped spread rumors that the United States had approved the use of not only the 20th Division but also the Special Warfare Command units.[19] This was untrue, except as within the context of the 20th Division decision. Unfortunately these false statements were not aggressively countered, a mistake that sowed the seeds of future anti-American sentiment.

The day before the ROK Army reentered Kwangju, Ambassador Gleysteen was asked indirectly by those resistors who were still occupying the provincial capitol if he would consent to act as a negotiator between them and the martial-law authorities. This was considered but eventually rejected by the ambassador because the ROK leaders had indicated that it was inappropriate for a person in Gleysteen's position to be so directly involved in what they considered an internal Korean matter.[20] Some embassy members, including myself, were disappointed that Gleysteen did not pursue this matter more vigorously. Of course, the Kwangju incident was an "internal" matter, but from a practical standpoint we had been closely involved in similar "internal" matters since 12/12 and had an obligation to do whatever we could to halt further bloodshed. Unfortunately the decision stood, and the army re-entered Kwangju the next morning, resulting in more casualties on both sides. This last fighting in the city was officially described as "well conducted" and with "light casualties"; in reality the struggle was fierce and numerous people were killed.

In my almost forty years of experience in dealing with Korea, the events in Kwangju of May, 1980, generate the saddest memories. Many times in the years to follow I wondered how we could have reacted differently and possibly had a better result. Clearly most of the blame for this terrible tragedy rests with Chun Doo Hwan and his martial-law group as well as a weak and easily manipulated ROK civilian government. But we Americans also deserve part of the blame. We should have acted more forcefully, especially at certain critical points. In the months following the 12/12 incident, we had an opportunity to act boldly, for the Chun group lacked legitimacy with the Korean people and with many in the government—even in the army. Instead, we tried to influence the situation through diplomacy and reason, but we were dealing with a people who only understood power and forcefulness. They had no qualms about twisting the Korean-American relationship, which to this point had been the strongest in the world, to their own advantage. After Kwangju, the relationship between South Korea and the United States was never the same.

Aftermath of Kwangju

Following the restoration of ROK government authority at Kwangju, the U.S. Embassy staff met to evaluate the new situation. As usual, there was some disagreement about what course our policy should now take. Although the final decisions would be made in Washington, our embassy evaluation and recommendations would be carefully considered in that process; therefore, these meetings were considered very important.

There had been occasional differences of opinion as to how to deal with the new group of self-appointed leaders of South Korea. In the past these disagreements had tended to be between the embassy and USFK, with the embassy focused on human rights and development of democracy and USFK concerned more about security posture and countering the North Korean threat. Following Kwangju, however, the division fell not so much along these lines, but more along age groups. The older embassy and USFK officials, who were relatively more senior in position and influence, seemed resigned to the fact that Chun and his group had successfully taken power, that despite our many attempts to urge a moderate course of action, we had failed. This group believed we now had few viable options remaining. Reluctantly, they were prepared to deal with Chun as the existing power.

The younger working-level staff members tended to be less analytical in their thinking and more emotional. They felt that there was still time to oppose Chun effectively if the embassy could develop a sound plan of action and convince Washington to aggressively support such a plan. We began to work on the details, but events were moving quickly.

On May 28 Ambassador Gleysteen sent his own evaluation to Washington.[21] This message essentially stated the obvious—that a small group of army officers had taken power step by step and that Korea was now under what amounted to a military occupation. He recounted in some detail earlier and unsuccessful efforts to persuade this group to follow a more democratic path. Gleysteen expressed his opinion that these efforts were totally discounted because the group had determined that the United States had no real options but to acquiesce—we would complain but take no real action. This appraisal was sent to Washington before the working-level embassy staff could put together a plan of action, and the result was to reinforce the position of the senior staff, who were now prepared to deal with Chun. Therefore, when the alternative plan was developed, there was a strong suspicion that it might already be too late.

Basically this draft plan had seven action elements designed to show in no uncertain terms where the U.S. government stood. First, we would aggressively censor and disavow Chun and his followers. If the U.S. government stood apart and did not support the 12/12 group, we believed, it would have a great influence. There were many anti-Chun groups within South Korea, and together they might gather strength if given support from the U.S. side. Obviously this would have been more effective earlier, but still it was not too late.

Second, instead of constantly complaining about press censorship and the continuing distortion of the American position, we would take independent action to get our message directly to the Korean people. Many of us had a wide and influential network of Korean friends and associates who could be approached independently and given the message that the United States did not support Chun and would support an open and fair election. We had the capability to deliver leaflets and handbills independently, but we instead depended on the martial-law authorities and official government outlets to deliver a message that was directly against their own interests and then complained when they failed to pass it along to the people.

Third, we would refuse any further contacts with Chun and his group. Instead, we actually upgraded these contacts, both in frequency and the level at which we met (as I will discuss soon). Every time one of these meetings occurred, it appeared to the Korean people that we were collaborating closely with the 12/12 group.

Fourth, every time a distortion concerning our true policy appeared, we would immediately counter it. According to an old proverb, "bad news does not improve with age." Yet in many cases we let distortions of our position remain unchallenged. We also failed to keep an accurate account of these false stories and, by the summer of 1980, had lost almost any official record of exactly what tales were being spread. Even the most ridiculous and unbelievable account will eventually gain some credibility if no one denies it, yet this was the situation we allowed to happen. It was not until 1989 that the U.S. government officially rebutted stories of American support for Chun's actions in 1980.[22]

Fifth, we would immediately withdraw both Ambassador Gleysteen and General Wickham from Korea, at least on a temporary basis, if not replace them altogether. This was not meant to be a criticism of their handling of the situation, for they were both good, capable, and honorable men who had tried to do the best they could under difficult conditions. By withdrawing them, however, a clear signal would be sent that we were opposed to Chun and his methods, and ordinary Koreans would know where we stood.

Sixth, we would take every opportunity in our contacts within the international community to censor Chun for his distortions of the American position, the imposition of martial law, and the events at Kwangju. For most of the time following Kwangju, our policy toward Chun was not even understood well within the international community in Seoul or by their governments at home. We had unrestricted access to these people, yet we did a poor job at mobilizing any opposition to Chun within the rest of the foreign diplomatic community.

Lastly, we should actively support the opposition political figures. To some extent this was done; however, much of our concern was expressed outside of Korea and tended to be concentrated only on Kim Dae Jung, who had powerful support abroad, particularly in the United States and Japan. The idea was not to support one particular individual, but the opposition as a whole as an alternative to Chun, with the objective of free elections.

None of these options were adopted, or as far as I know even presented, to the ambassador, much less forwarded to Washington.[23] Instead, a series of policy meetings began in Washington at the end of May and continued into late June.[24] These meetings were ultimately unsatisfactory at developing any significant policy changes. The Carter administration did not want to send any signals that would imply support for Chun and the generals, yet it was reluctant to take the type of firm actions that were necessary to express direct opposition. Eventually it decided to take a "cool and aloof" public stance while at the same time privately urging Chun to resume constitutional reform and move toward democratic elections.

A major reason that these meetings produced such a mild and ineffective result was the manner in which they were conducted. Because any decision on our Korea policy would necessarily involve security, foreign policy, economic, and other considerations, several departments of the government were involved. Although the State Department had the lead role in determining the agenda and chairing the meetings, the Defense Department actually played the dominant role. Other departments and agencies such as Commerce and the CIA were also involved. I had participated previously in many of these interagency meetings. Because of the different viewpoints and concerns of each agency, I had little confidence that they would reach a satisfactory result. The customary approach was that, when one agency objected to a particular course of action, it was usually "watered down." The outcome was what we called the "lowest common denominator" solution, which is the option to which the fewest people objected and that was the least controversial. This is what happened in the aftermath of Kwangju, and it resulted in a continued weak and ineffective Korea policy.

Gleysteen Meets Chun after Kwangju

Following instructions, Ambassador Gleysteen met with Chun Doo Hwan at least twice in June, 1980.[25] At the first meeting early in the month, Gleysteen told Chun that the United States had great concern over events since full martial law had been declared and suggested that some sort of statement of regret over the events at Kwangju should be issued. At the second meeting he presented American views on the best way to reconcile relations between South Korea and the United States. These were to end martial law and to move toward political liberalization and elections, which were by now well-known suggestions to the Korean side. Gleysteen also raised for the first time his concern that it would be difficult to sustain the previously strong security and economic relationship between our two countries without progress on domestic Korean political issues. He further complained about misinformation that had been broadcast concerning the American role at Kwangju and the anti-Americanism that had resulted. Chun downplayed the anti-Americanism issue, blaming it on a few radicals.

In July Gleysteen met with Chun once more, this time to complain about misuse of the ROK-U.S. security relationship in order to advance the general's own political ambitions. There is no evidence that any of these meetings resulted in any positive results from the American viewpoint. In fact, since the American ambassador was now meeting him regularly, they tended to legitimize Chun's authority.

Throughout the period, the Carter administration's interest was diverted from Korea due to other problems, particularly in the Middle East. A number of American diplomats had been taken hostage by the regime of the Ayatollah Khomeini in Iran, and this issue consumed the Carter administration.[26] Also, the presidential election campaign was heating up, and Republican Ronald Reagan represented a formidable challenge to Carter's reelection hopes.[27] It began to take more time to get policy guidance and answers from Washington on matters concerning Korea, and it was becoming clear that the peninsula was now of less interest than developments in the Middle East, particularly Iran. Basically we were told to do the best we could within existing policy guidelines. "Don't call us; we'll call you" was the message from home.

The Second Countercoup Plot

In late June we once again began to hear rumors of a possible countercoup among some members of the Korean military. This time, the center of the dissatisfaction was not in the Class 8 group, which by then had faded from any position of authority in the army. Instead, it appeared to be a group of younger officers, including some who were members of the Special Warfare Command. According to several reports, members of this group felt that they had been used improperly during the Kwangju incident and were now being made into scapegoats for that tragic event. According to these men, some of whom had personally participated in those events, their units had been told that the Kwangju resistors were Communists and under the direct influence of North Korea. This propaganda by their own leaders apparently played a big part in the overreaction by the special-warfare forces in the city. Basically these men felt that their leadership had misled them about the Kwangju situation and the motivation of the resistors. Now their national leaders were not supporting them adequately while the special-warfare units were being widely criticized.

I know that Colonel Blottie was being briefed on this situation regularly and that Bob Brewster also was informed. I believe that the situation was ultimately resolved by the Korean Army itself, without any confrontation or bloodshed but with some reasoning with the group and using strong leadership skills. Some "troublemaking" personnel may have been transferred as well. As far as I know, the American side played no role in this at all, at most only passive listening. Obviously, even had this not been the case, we would have discouraged any countercoup for many of the same reasons that we had discouraged it during the previous anti-Chun rumors in January.

The Trial of Kim Dae Jung

Of the opposition politicians who had been arrested, Kim Dae Jung was the best known internationally. There was great concern over his fate, and we at the embassy were under strong pressure to monitor his situation.[28] The military authorities brought him to trial on charges that appeared to be weak and perhaps even fabricated. After numerous protests, we were allowed to have an embassy observer at the trial, and he came to the conclusion that the evidence against Kim was far too weak to justify a death sentence. The U.S. government issued a statement calling the charges against the dissident "farfetched" and was somewhat successful at directing international concern. After Chun Doo Hwan became president in August, direct and prolonged negotiations began over Kim's fate. In mid-September the court sentenced Kim to death, and Chun maneuvered skillfully on the matter to gain full and formal acceptance of his presidency. Early in the Reagan administration, he was invited to Washington in return for the commutation of Kim Dae Jung's sentence to life imprisonment.[29] Chun had been successful in blackmailing the United States, and from that time forward our relations were essentially normalized.

Why the Carter Policy Failed

By the summer of 1980, the U.S. government had resigned itself to the fact that Chun Doo Hwan and his followers were the future political leadership of South Korea. Despite endless meetings and numerous attempts to encourage political liberalization, this policy had failed. Some of the reasons for this failure are by now obvious, but let me summarize them.

First, we allowed our fear of North Korea to dominate our policy decisions, perhaps in part as an overreaction to the recent furor over intelligence estimates and U.S. troop withdrawals. In reality, North Korea should have been only a minor concern. To be sure, we believed its military to be a powerful and dangerous force, but even in 1979–80 it was evident that the ROK was far outstripping the North in almost every measure of national power, including international recognition, economic development, and others. We ignored these developments as well as the fact that North Korea gave no signs of initiating aggressive military action. In this way, we put stability ahead of democracy and became a hostage of our own Korea policy. By concentrating so much on maintaining stability, we allowed the North Koreans to influence our policy in the South, even though they never were a real factor in any of the events of 1979–80.

Also, I believe some senior U.S. government officials had a fear that Korea might disintegrate the way Vietnam and Iran had during the same timeframe. To those of us who knew Korea well, this was very unlikely, but to certain policymakers in Washington, the warning signs in Korea were similar to Iran. They were prepared to live with another military regime before they would take a chance of further instability. In this regard, the Kwangju incident had truly shaken the confidence of the Carter government.

Not all the mistakes were made in Washington. Neither the U.S. Embassy nor USFK fully appreciated the ambitious nature of the KMA Class 11 group, despite early and continuing reports. After 12/12, USFK spent far too much time and effort complaining about proper CFC OPCON procedures. These resources would have been better used in other ways, for example, linking our security commitment with the ongoing support of the American people, who were more apt to approve of a democratic government in South Korea than another military dictatorship. But USFK's considerable influence with the ROK military was never used to its full potential—perhaps because of institutional jealousy and the embassy's desire to be "in charge" of something that it could never really control.

Neither Gleysteen nor Wickham talked to the right people. The ambassador had a strong staff, including some experienced Korea hands such as Spence Richardson in the political section and myself. We were infrequently consulted, except by officials below Gleysteen. General Wickham's staff was largely out of the loop. The general ran most of the show himself, even though he was not knowledgeable about Korea. In addition, he was frequently out of the country, often at critical times. Aware after 12/12 that he was being criticized in Washington, Wickham may have wanted to shore up his base at home.[30]

We also missed some opportunities. Had we had a more focused administration in Washington and less-cautious leadership in Korea, we might have made a stronger attempt to work closely with the military moderates after the Park assassination, taken a stronger anti-Chun posture immediately after 12/12, or even as late as the end of May, 1980, in accordance with the plan suggested by some of the younger embassy members. Clearly the earlier the action had been taken, the better the prospects for its success. Once Chun had seized control of the army, the chance for early democratization dimmed considerably. These prospects did not disappear, however, and had the United States chosen a bolder course, democracy might have blossomed nearly a decade earlier than it actually did. At the very least the United States would have communicated its views to the Korean people in a manner that would have averted many of the hard feelings that linger to this day.

CHAPTER 10

Return to the United States

I n the summer of 1980, my normal three-year assignment with the U.S. Embassy in Seoul was coming to an end. I had been asked to stay for an additional year but instead requested transfer to a field unit in Korea. By this time I had spent almost nine continuous years in the Korean intelligence and high-level policy business, and I was anxious to return to more traditional military duties. In late summer, therefore, I was assigned as executive officer of a communications brigade and spent the next year working on problems of operations, maintenance, personnel, and all the similar concerns of the typical military unit.

It was quite enjoyable duty. Among other things, I was able to fly all over South Korea by helicopter, which evoked thoughts of changes that had occurred in the countryside over the past generation. The predominantly rural and undeveloped landscape of the early 1960s had been replaced by a more urbanized setting, and the transportation network was especially modernized. Where private autos had once been rare, they were now common. This transition, which in most countries takes two or three generations, had happened in the ROK in less than twenty years. Unfortunately my job assignment only lasted one year, which went by very quickly, and I was reassigned stateside in the summer of 1981.

Back to School

My new assignment was as a faculty member at the U.S. Army Command and General Staff College (CGSC) at Fort Leavenworth, Kansas. This school was and still is highly selective; only the army's most promising officers are selected for attendance. In addition to the U.S. Army officers, who formed the majority of students, we had students from the U.S. Air Force, Navy, and Marine Corps and over one hundred foreign officers from about forty different countries. Included in the international student body each year were several South Koreans, and I found myself in especially close contact with these officers because of my previous experience and background.

Most of the foreign officers were the best from their country. Many went on to become generals and even chiefs of staff of their respective national services. In Korea, for example, both former Army Chief of Staff Kim Jin Young and former Chairman of the Joint Chiefs of Staff and later Minister of Defense Kim Dong Jin were graduates, and former Minister of Defense Rhee Byong Tae was a graduate of both the CGSC and the even more prestigious U.S. Army War College at Carlisle Barracks, Pennsylvania. There are other examples as well.

The primary purpose of the CGSC was to teach professional military subjects such as tactics, logistics, command, leadership, and strategy. I was assigned to the strategy department and placed in charge of the Asia curriculum. We taught geopolitics, strategy formulation, international relations, and similar subjects. Most of the student officers were at the rank of major and had not been exposed to these subjects before, so there was a high interest.

Although the CGSC had what was probably the finest military curriculum in the world, I was dissatisfied about one thing. Each year about thirty new CGSC graduates were assigned to duties in Korea immediately following graduation. These officers were among the best in the U.S. Army, but few had been to Korea previously or knew anything about the culture, history, language, combined ROK-U.S. military system, or any of the other things that were unique to the region. Building on the work of my predecessor, Lt. Col. Don Boose, who was also a Korea expert, I asked the college commandant to authorize an expanded course of instruction especially for these students. As designed, this course would be given during the last semester and would be ten weeks in duration. Such a course could not make instant Korea experts of the students, but it could produce officers who were ready to effectively serve almost immediately after arriving, instead of spending several weeks adjusting to the country. This was particularly important because many of the officers assigned to Korea were there for only one year, so there was a real need for them to be productive from the very beginning of their assignment.

It was at first difficult to get approval to expand this course; not only was it a new idea but also there was no such course for any other country. For example, each year more than one hundred CGSC graduates were ordered to West Germany, yet there was no special course for any of those officers. I argued long and hard that Korea was not the same as Europe, that military duty in Korea was quite different from duty in Europe because of the sharper disparities in culture and language and the more complex command relationships. Eventually the expanded course was approved, and we added sections on the organization and structure of the Korean armed forces, the peninsular defense plan, and a tactical exercise designed to test all newly acquired information in a practical application. That was in 1982, and the Korea orientation course is still being taught today. I am told that Korea is still the only country with its own course at the CGSC.

After two years as an instructor, I was selected for promotion to full colonel and put in charge of the Joint and Combined Operations Committee, which included not only a core curriculum on joint-combined operations but courses on Europe and the Middle East as well. Korea remained my first love, however, and I was the only full colonel on the faculty who continued to teach as well as be an administrator and manager.

Return to Washington

In the early spring of 1985, I was asked by the office of then Assistant Secretary of Defense Richard Armitage to work on a special project involving Korea.[1] I was told that this project would be very important to our future security relationship with the ROK. Immediately accepting this assignment, in the summer I reported to the Office of the Secretary of Defense in Washington.

Pentagon duty in 1985 was not much different than it had been when I was assigned there in 1972. The building was still old, dusty, and impersonal. As a colonel I had my own office, but it was very small, consisting of a desk and chair, one chair for a visitor, and a large wall safe for document storage. I had enjoyed much better office space as a major and lieutenant colonel but was determined to make do with the situation.

To grasp the importance of this study to the U.S. Department of Defense, it must be understood that our defense policy toward Korea had not changed significantly in almost thirty years. Since the mid-1950s we had maintained forces in South Korea with basically the same objective and with very little alteration of command relationships. U.S. ground forces were reduced by one infantry division in the early 1970s, and the Combined Forces Command was formed in 1978, but no other major changes had occurred. The Department of Defense wanted to reevaluate this relationship for the future, not in terms of the basic commitment to Korea's security, which was firm and secured by treaty obligation, but in terms of the present and projected threat from North Korea, the growing economic disparity between North and South, the organization of the CFC, the relative roles and responsibilities of each country, and other issues (for example, the continuation of the joint military training exercise Team Spirit).

This study took over a year to produce, and some of the conclusions were controversial. For instance, the evaluation of the North Korean threat had not been revised significantly since the army study sponsored by General Aaron in 1975, some ten years earlier. During those ten years, a lot had changed on the peninsula. While the North remained a serious military threat, it was becoming questionable whether its poor economy could in fact support and sustain a modern war. By using a series of computer projections and economic models, it became obvious that North Korea could only continue to maintain its large military machine by further neglecting its economy. I concluded that, if the current trends continued, by the mid-1990s North Korea would probably no longer be able to adequately maintain its large conventional force.[2] Although this estimate was probably accurate, what I did not consider or know at the time was that someone in Pyongyang was probably reaching a similar conclusion and that the seeds of the North Korean nuclear program were likely being planted as a result.[3] (That issue, however, is very complicated, and I will discuss it in more detail a little later.)

Besides an updated threat evaluation, there was the matter of the proper relationship between the ROK and U.S. forces, particularly an examination of what roles and responsibilities were appropriate for each country. In the 1950s and 1960s, for example, it was logical, for a number of reasons, to have a U.S. general exercise operational control over both ROK and U.S. forces. By the 1970s we had moved to a more integrated and binational command structure under the CFC arrangement. For the 1990s, I believed a more modern arrangement was appropriate, with Korea taking the lead in security matters and the United States moving to a supporting role. The U.S. strength was in its air power, which was far superior to the North Korean air forces, and its logistical system, which could deliver the large amounts of fuel, ammunition, and other supplies necessary to wage war successfully. The ROK had excellent light infantry, a good defense/industrial base, and a well-rehearsed strategy for defense. The task at hand was to ensure that each partner focused on its respective strengths. Later this initiative became adopted as official policy and was known to the Americans as the "leading to supporting role" policy.

In addition to focusing on each other's strengths, the study recommendations called for the South Koreans to take the overall lead in most security matters relating to the peninsula, a goal to be accomplished on a gradual timetable. This meant several first steps were in order. One of these was changing the senior member of the United Nations Military Armistice Commission from an American to a Korean general, which was finally acted upon in 1991.[4] At the time it was mostly a symbolic change, but it is inappropriate to my way of thinking to have an American as the senior negotiator at Panmunjom facing the North Koreans. The North did not respond or formally recognize this change to a "Korean face," but at least we made the important point that the Koreans were ultimately in charge of their own security, with the Americans backing them up—not the other way around.

Another study recommendation was that a Korean general be appointed as commander of the ground forces component of the CFC. This has also finally been implemented. It was inappropriate for an American officer to command the ground forces, which were almost entirely Korean soldiers. I also proposed that operational control of Korean forces be returned to South Korea in peacetime, which was not actually carried out until 1994.

At some time in the future, the day may also come when the nationality of the CFC commander himself is changed from an American to a Korean general. There are sensitive political considerations involved on both sides on this issue, but to my way of thinking, South Korea can never move to a true leading role until this is done. There is no valid military reason to wait any longer, although there are cogent political and deterrent reasons.

The 1986 study also addressed the annual Team Spirit military exercise. For several years, North Korea had demanded cancellation of Team Spirit, calling it provocative. Nothing of the sort was true since it was essentially a defensive type of exercise. The ROK-U.S. side even went so far as to invite North Korea to send its own observers to Team Spirit in order to verify this fact, but that government consistently refused. The study recommendation was that Team Spirit be continued for as long as the ROK and U.S. governments felt it contributed to security in Korea.[5]

Not all of my Pentagon assignment was spent chained to my desk. From time to time I was able to return to South Korea on business related either to the study or other policy matters. Also, I worked closely with Wally Knowles, a longtime fixture in the Pentagon, who was the assistant for Korea at the time. Wally was an old friend with whom I had worked closely during my earlier years on the army staff. Most of our collaboration was on security-consultative-meeting issues, and we made a good team, occasionally traveling to Korea together on meeting-related business.

These visits gave me a good sense of events in Korea, primarily on the military side, where the Korean-American relationship remained strong despite the trauma of the 12/12 incident and subsequent events. Among the general Korean public, however, I sensed a sullen attitude that was different from previous times. Some of this I attributed to resentment of the continuing authoritarian practices of the Chun Doo Hwan government. There was also, however, a strong undercurrent of anti-American feeling. This unfortunate development was fueled by several factors, among which were continuing suspicions concerning our role during 12/12 and the subsequent Kwangju tragedy, trade friction, and an occasionally hostile Korean press, which sometimes seemed determined to distort U.S. policies and actions. Anti-American sentiment would continue to be a factor in the years ahead.

Military-Attaché Training

Following the complete staffing and acceptance of most of the study recommendations, I was notified that I would be assigned to the Defense Intelligence Agency for further assignment as the defense attaché in Seoul. This would be my fourth assignment to Korea, and I eagerly looked forward to it.

By now DIA had developed a school for prospective attachés. This was required training for everyone except myself, for I had already served as a military attaché. Because the alternative was another six months in the Pentagon, however, I quickly volunteered for the attaché training course, followed by some Korean-language refresher training.

The attaché course was interesting and enjoyable, and we were able to listen to many guest lectures from senior officials in the Washington area and take field trips to interesting places in the United States. There was a course on antiterrorism, for example, where we learned to escape an ambush, avoid a kidnapping attempt, and other James Bond–type activities. This was not necessary for assignment to South Korea, of course, but some of our military attachés and diplomats had previously been assassinated or kidnapped in Europe and the Middle East, so we all received such training. They also had a short course for our wives since they were expected to do a lot of entertaining and also be a representative of their country. All in all, it was a very enjoyable time and not very demanding, and when it was time to depart once again for Korea, we were refreshed and ready.

CHAPTER 11

My Fourth Tour in Korea Begins

I arrived back in Korea in August, 1987, with my wife and youngest son; by now my two oldest sons were no longer living with us, one being an army officer stationed in Hawaii, and the other attending college on the U.S. mainland. The defense attaché was always assigned the same house on Yongsan South Post, and within a few days we were reasonably settled in our new quarters and were adjusting once more to diplomatic life in Seoul.

In contrast to my first two assignments to the U.S. Embassy, which were concerned primarily with training and situation reporting, this time my duties were more managerial. The Defense Attaché Office, which was only one officer and an administrative assistant when I was attached there in 1972 as a foreign-area-officer student, had expanded by 1987.[1] In addition to the defense attaché, who was in overall charge, there were now principal attachés representing the air force and navy, two assistant attachés for the army (since it was the largest service in Korea), and a four-person administrative staff.

As was the case during the 12/12 incident and following events, we worked closely with the embassy's Political Section, the Office of the Special Assistant to the Ambassador, and increasingly with the embassy's Commercial Section. This latter relationship was because of the growing importance of Korea as an economic partner and the increasing importance that trade and other economic matters held in our nations' official relationship.

My counterpart in the Political Section was Charles Kartman, the political counselor. Chuck, as we called him, had a very young appearance and was sometimes mistaken for a junior officer. In fact, he had a reputation as one of the brightest stars in the State Department and had been promoted very rapidly. We got along quite well together; even when we were on opposite sides of some issues, I always had the greatest respect for his views and opinions.[2]

The special assistant to the ambassador in 1987 was John Stein. John had been with the CIA for many years and had already held very senior positions in Washington. We became very close professionally as well as personally (and although we are both now retired, we still communicate regularly). John was very competent and highly respected in Washington. It was a measure of the importance the U.S. government attached to Korea that John Stein was assigned to Seoul, for he was truly the best in his field.

The ambassador was James Lilley, a China expert whose first love remained that country. In 1974–75 he had worked directly for George Bush when the future president was chief liaison officer in Beijing.[3] Ambassador Lilley, of course, was very interested in Washington politics and especially the presidential election, which would occur the following year. Most of us expected that George Bush, the Republican candidate, would appoint him to an important position in Washington or as ambassador to China if he was elected in 1988. Like Bush, Lilley had a long career in the U.S. government and had served in a variety of policy positions in the State Department and with the CIA. Tall, self-confident, and forceful, he fit well into Korea's masculine style of politics. He was smart, knowledgeable, and had numerous contacts, a very effective ambassador at a crucial moment in Korean-American relations.

The commander of Combined Forces Command and U.S. Forces Korea was Gen. Louis Menetrey. I had known the general earlier while on the U.S. Army Command and General Staff College faculty at Fort Leavenworth as well as when he was commander of the ROK-U.S. Combined Field Army at Uijongbu. He was an excellent field soldier and, now on his third assignment to South Korea, knew the country well.

Although we got along well personally, General Menetrey was not entirely satisfied with the way my office was organized. My job, in addition to providing advice and support to the ambassador on military affairs, was to report directly to Defense Intelligence Agency headquarters in Washington items of interest on the military situation, particularly to keep the U.S. government informed about the ROK military. This meant that to some extent the general and I had overlapping responsibilities. The difference was that his responsibilities, in addition to being broader, were in the operational area, whereas mine were oriented more toward intelligence. General Menetrey was concerned that the attachés would be reporting matters of interest to the DIA without these being coordinated or cleared through his headquarters, and soon after my arrival, he sent for me to discuss these matters.

At this meeting in his office at CFC headquarters, Menetrey was clear and firm in his wishes. He wanted all significant reporting on military matters to go through his command. Also, he expected me to function as a liaison officer between the embassy and USFK and to keep him and his staff informed as to what the embassy's position and strategy were on key issues in which the views of the State and Defense Departments might differ. Finally, he wanted to replace, or at least "assist," the ambassador as my rating officer for evaluation purposes—in other words, to be directly involved in the annual evaluation of how well I did my job.

It is not easy for a colonel to directly disagree with a four-star general, but I felt an obligation to do so. At this point I had little expectation of reaching general rank in the army; my primary ambition was simply to do as good a job as possible in my current assignment. My duty was clear, I explained to Menetrey, and that was to support the ambassador, who was my direct boss in South Korea, and the director of the DIA, who was my boss in Washington. I described our intelligence-reporting channel and explained the reasons that we required direct field reporting to our headquarters rather than through USFK. As politely as possible, I refused his request.

General Menetrey was still dissatisfied and subsequently sent a message to my boss, a three-star general in Washington. Fortunately my boss supported my position, and I continued to function completely independent of USFK. Later there were some significant policy disagreements between USFK and the embassy, and I was happy I was not caught in the middle.

The ROK Presidential Campaign and Election

When I arrived back in Seoul, the big political news was Roh Tae Woo's call for free and open elections to determine the next president of South Korea.[4] Roh was Chun Doo Hwan's designated successor. Initially Chun seemed determined that Roh would be selected by a sort of electoral college, the membership of which would be stacked in his favor. On June 29, however, Roh announced that the choice would be by popular election. This news was roundly applauded throughout the country. The U.S. government also was delighted, for it had been encouraging such a move for a long time. Indeed, the upcoming election campaign would occupy most of the U.S. Embassy's time until the end of the year.

Just as the 1987 election was a milestone in modern Korean history, it was also a milestone for American policy on the peninsula. In Washington there had been an ongoing debate for several years concerning the best way to convince the Chun government that open elections were in its best interest. During the Carter years, direct and continuous confrontation with the

ROK military authorities had not produced any good result. The Reagan policy was to continue to encourage liberalization of the Korean political system, though in a less confrontational and demanding manner. During the time that Ambassador Richard L. Walker was in Seoul (1981–86), he had met privately with Roh Tae Woo and his associates on a regular basis. Walker was a very low-key, yet skillful, diplomat, and I think his softer approach to the issue of free elections made some impression on Roh.[5] Both Lilley, who replaced Walker in the fall of 1986, and Assistant Secretary of State for East Asian and Pacific Affairs Gaston Sigur in Washington were determined to avoid a repeat of the course of events of 1980. They maneuvered skillfully to achieve this goal.

My own opinion is that Chun's and Roh's decision to support a free and open election was caused by several practical factors, not the least of which was that Roh thought he stood a better than 50-50 chance of winning. Kim Jong Pil, Kim Dae Jung, and Kim Young Sam were sure to divide the opposition vote, and this would give Roh an excellent opportunity to win a plurality, which was all that was needed to win the election under the proposed reforms. Also, he faced the prospect of continuous demonstrations, even violent civil conflict, if he refused, for unrest was far more widespread than it had been in 1980. I suspect that American views may have had some part in the military government's decision, but they were certainly not the major factor. Regardless, our diplomatic overtures on this subject were certainly handled more adeptly by the Reagan administration than by Carter. They included successful efforts to convey the U.S. belief that the armed forces should not intervene in the internal political or civil affairs of the country.

In September, 1987, Ambassador Lilley was instructed by Washington that the successful conduct of the presidential election represented the American government's number-one policy objective in Korea in the weeks ahead. Although it was not directly stated, it was understood that if the military stayed out of the election and honored its results, our policy would be considered successful. From that time on, Lilley was totally focused on this subject. He met with Chuck Kartman, John Stein, and me at least weekly to discuss election issues. The election was also the major topic during the weekly country-team meeting, which included all the principal embassy staff. Lilley was especially interested in what the Korean military was thinking and whether or not they would stay out of the political arena this time and allow the voting to proceed.

My view of the Korean military in the fall of 1987 was that it had changed considerably since 1979–80. I had always viewed Roh Tae Woo as more moderate than Chun and believed that the army would follow his leadership and respect the outcome of the election. There were, of course, some hard-line officers who liked the old system better, but they kept their views to themselves for the most part. My feeling was that the Korean people would not stand for another military government, that the military knew and respected this fact, and that the election would proceed on schedule.[6]

The thing that concerned most of us in the embassy was not the process itself, but the possible outcome. Specifically, what would the armed forces do if Kim Dae Jung was elected? My analysis was that the military clearly favored a Roh victory but that they would accept an alternative winner such as Kim Young Sam without causing any problem. There was some sympathy for Kim Dae Jung among some of the embassy staff, particularly the younger officers, but we were careful to approach the election in a totally neutral way, using facts and not emotions to reach our judgments. In this way, both John Stein and I believed that there was a greater-than-even chance of the military refusing to accept a Kim Dae Jung victory. We began to prepare an informal reaction plan in the event he was elected.

This plan, which was never finalized or adopted as policy, called for the U.S. government to take an active role to influence the ROK military to respect the election results regardless of who won. The elements of this plan were that the U.S. government would immediately announce, in both Washington and Seoul, its unqualified support for the newly elected president. The ambassador would then congratulate the winner immediately in a well-publicized meeting to demonstrate our support. There would also be strong statements issued in both Washington and Seoul, simultaneously, directed against any military intervention. This plan proved unnecessary since Roh Tae Woo won the election, but I believe it would have been implemented aggressively if there had been a different outcome.

Ambassador Lilley, in addition to being very concerned over the possibility of military intervention, was determined that the embassy not be perceived to favor one candidate over another. There were rumors that the U.S. government supported Roh because we thought he would be more acceptable to the military and thus would ensure stability. The truth is that we had no favorite candidate officially, but I believe we would have been least comfortable with Kim Dae Jung. Of course, we would have supported him as indicated before, but most of us were secretly relieved when he did not win. Anyhow, Lilley preached to all the embassy staff on a regular basis the importance of maintaining our neutrality and not to make any comments that would be interpreted as supporting a particular candidate.

In this regard, one day shortly before the election, the ambassador was presiding over the weekly country-team meeting. This particular day he was especially concerned about the neutrality issue and talked about it at some length. By the time he finished, everyone in the meeting was very aware of how important Lilley considered this subject, and we were convinced that anyone who violated this neutrality order would probably be sent home in disgrace. Immediately after the meeting, Lilley had an appointment with a certain retired Korean brigadier general, whom I went to greet and to escort him into the ambassador's office. When we entered the office's reception area, the general busily began trying to pass out Roh Tae Woo campaign buttons and campaign literature to several embarrassed embassy staffers. Fortunately Ambassador Lilley had ducked into the restroom and missed most of this event. We later joked about it, although I doubt he thought it funny at the time.

A few days before the election, I took a trip to the southern area of Korea to see Kim Jin Young, who by now was a major general in charge of the ROK Army's Third Military Academy. This was not considered a very good assignment for a major general, especially one who had received such rapid promotions as Kim. But he had been involved in some controversy while a division commander, and the conventional wisdom was that he was now in disfavor. I did not really believe this was true, but in any case, I had always valued his friendship and was anxious to see him again. We had a good visit, a tour of the academy, and enjoyed lunch with his staff officers.

Later that evening we met at a Korean-style restaurant for a private dinner. I was the host and had arranged for an excellent meal with hostesses, music, and typical entertainment. General Kim was not interested in these, however, so we ate alone quietly. This was not unusual, for he was a strong Christian and seldom drank much, unlike some generals who frequently enjoyed such parties. Instead, we discussed the upcoming election, our families, and other such matters.

Kim Jin Young asked me who the embassy thought would win the election. After emphasizing our neutrality, I replied that the Political Section believed Kim Young Sam would win, but my office and others believed that Roh would come out on top because the three Kims would split the opposition vote. "You are correct," the general said. "Roh will win." I sensed at that time that General Kim believed he was personally vulnerable if Kim Young Sam or another candidate besides Roh won. (This turned out to be the case, of course, but not for over five years, when he was prematurely and abruptly removed as army chief of staff by Kim Young Sam.)

The official estimate of the embassy's Political Section on the 1987 election, which projected Kim Young Sam as the winner, was based on some polling data that it had monitored, which was supposedly done very scientifically. It came as quite a surprise and embarrassment to them when Roh was declared the winner. The day after the election, there was a report that the results had been tampered with, but there was no hard evidence to back such a claim.[7] Anyhow, the embassy was relieved and happy that the election had been successful and that South Korea had moved another step closer to full democracy. Ambassador Lilley was especially relieved that the military had not intervened.

The Olympics

Just as 1988 was a special year for Korea, so was it for Americans who were lucky enough to be in Seoul for the 1988 Olympic Games. I accompanied my family to many of the events, including the Opening Ceremonies. It was quite a thrill and a spectacular show. I cannot remember any Olympics before or since that was organized or performed any better.

Our major professional concern during preparations for the games was counterterrorism.[8] We had indications as early as the spring of 1986 that the North would probably make trouble. It began with an increased propaganda campaign, which included stepped-up charges of armistice violations and the creation of several incidents along the DMZ. In March and April came false charges that Seoul had eleven thousand cases of AIDS and attempts to inflate student demonstrations, which the North portrayed as violent and dangerous to foreigners. This type of activity escalated throughout 1986 and 1987, culminating in the "Mayumi" bombing of a Korean Airlines flight from the Middle East to Seoul in November, 1987.[9] By early 1988 we were receiving reports indicating that the North Koreans might be planning even more disasters in a desperate attempt to sabotage the Olympics.

As always the South Koreans and Americans worked very closely, especially on intelligence, to ensure a terrorist-free Olympics. The details of the specific actions taken to counter any further North Korean plots are to some extent still secret. They included, though, a full-scale and greatly expanded intelligence watch, the creation of a twenty-four-hour crisis-response cell that was poised to react immediately, and the positioning of additional U.S. strategic military assets within easy retaliatory distance of North Korea. Further, there was a certain direct message passed to the North that made it absolutely clear that any attempt to disrupt a peaceful Olympics would result in a swift and decisive counteraction. I believe these detailed preparations and actions helped produce second thoughts in North Korea about disrupting the games.

During and following the Olympics, we had a steady stream of VIPs who visited South Korea. I was able to meet and talk with several of these, including former Presidents Nixon and Ford, Henry Kissinger, and several others. Seoul in those days was almost like Hollywood, there were so many celebrities. My wife worked for NBC VIP relations during the Olympics and was able to meet and guide the movie star Arnold Schwarzenegger around the capital. Even though she also was able to meet Nixon, Ford, Kissinger, and numerous other VIPs, she was impressed the most by Schwarzenegger—she still talks about "her friend Arnold."

Despite our cooperation and assistance in helping make the Olympics a success, this was also a period of rising anti-Americanism in Korea. The causes of this sentiment were complex then and remain so today. Koreans were understandably proud that they hosted such a successful Olympics and were angered at some of the unflattering coverage by the American media, especially NBC's treatment of an incident involving a Korean boxer. The Olympics also enhanced their nationalism, and several unfortunate events involving Americans during the Olympics only added fuel to the fire.[10]

Following the games, Ambassador Lilley's attention focused directly on the U.S. presidential election. As a close associate of George Bush, he was far from neutral in the contest. When Bush was elected in November, 1988, Lilley was delighted and began plans to leave his post in Seoul. Most of us thought he would be named ambassador to China, but I think Lilley himself would have preferred a job in Washington, possibly as national security advisor. Bush eventually assigned him to China. Late in the administration, Lilley served in a senior Pentagon post.

Intelligence Failures

Although our information about North Korea was generally good during this period, there were at least two incidents where it was inaccurate. The first was the erroneously reported death of Kim Il Sung in November, 1986.[11]

This mistake was an example of what happens when rumors become public before the intelligence apparatus has an opportunity to fully evaluate them. The rumor that Kim Il Sung had died apparently began with a newspaper report from Tokyo. That in itself should have caused suspicion, for Japanese press reports on matters concerning the Korean peninsula often tended to be alarmist and unsubstantiated. This particular story took on a life of its own. Shortly following the Japanese report, a front-line ROK unit reported that the North Koreans were playing somber music, and there was an unconfirmed report that the flag of North Korea at its truce village near Panmunjom was flying at half-mast. Neither of these reports proved to be true, but they were immediately reported by the media. The Korean intelligence community tended to believe the rumors, while the U.S. side was unable to provide any confirmation. We had received the same reports regarding the flag and music but could not determine their accuracy. Unfortunately, either through a misunderstanding, translation error, or perhaps because of intense pressure from the Blue House to either confirm or deny this story, the Korean Ministry of Defense reported publicly that Kim Il Sung was indeed dead. It was quite an embarrassment when he showed up the following day to greet a Mongolian delegation at the Pyongyang airport, looking healthy and fit.

Another intelligence fiasco was Kumgang Dam. South Koreans, based on engineering studies and some defector reports, strongly believed that the North Korean Kumgang Dam project was designed for military rather than civilian purposes. If completed, they believed the structure could release millions of tons of water that would flood areas of the South. In response, they began construction on a counterdam called the "Peace Dam."[12] The American side was under a lot of pressure from the Korean side to confirm the threatening nature of the Kumgang Dam. Despite many weeks of study, we were never able to verify the extent of danger actually posed. Because our Korean allies were so concerned and had spent a great deal of effort and money on the "Peace Dam," we eventually supported their claims, although there really was not much evidence to confirm them.

If there is a common point to these two incidents, it is that, to be effective and reliable, intelligence must always make its judgments completely independent of political pressure. Otherwise there will invariably be mistakes or inaccurate information released. In my experience, it is better to admit you are not certain about a particular situation than it is to pretend you have all the answers. This is especially true in the international-intelligence business, where wrong judgments can have very serious consequences.

Visiting Congressmen

One of the sources of political pressure on American officials in the field has always been visiting congressmen from Washington, who in my experience often had a rather negative view of Korean leaders and of U.S. Embassy personnel. For better or for worse, many congressmen visiting Korea on official business actually spent most of their time engaging in other activities. Some were even so bold as to go from Kimpo Airport directly to the Itaewon district for intensive shopping sprees. At times they canceled previous appointments with Korean officials for highly questionable reasons.

One frequent visitor to Korea was a certain New York congressman who always insisted on seeing his tailor immediately upon arrival, regardless of the time, day or night. The tailor never complained since he was making money, but often times the embassy staff who were required to escort this politician grew frustrated and angry.

Another congressman was rumored to have a girlfriend in Seoul. Usually he went directly to his hotel on arrival, came out about two days later complaining about "jet lag," received a perfunctory briefing at the embassy, and then returned to his hotel room for another two days. (Although we resented his waste of taxpayer money, we certainly did admire his stamina.)

A certain high-level State Department official was another frequent visitor. This person had difficulty finding shoes that fit correctly, so he usually had two or three pairs custom made when he visited Korea. During one such trip, on his first day in Seoul, he went to a shoemaker in Itaewon, picked out the shoe designs, had his foot measured, and paid a substantial deposit. When he was ready to depart later in the week, his aide returned to the shoe store to pick up his order. Unfortunately the assistant could not locate the store again. After looking for some time, he called the embassy in a near panic, asking assistance. Even with such help, the store was never located. It later turned out that the store had suddenly changed owners that same week and was now selling sweatsuits instead of shoes. For almost six months, we received messages from this VIP and his staff inquiring about his shoes, but without any satisfactory results.

One popular destination for visiting congressmen was the "Third North Korean Tunnel" north of Munsan. This was an infiltration tunnel excavated by the North Koreans for military purposes. Being reasonably close to Seoul, it attracted many tourists, including numerous VIPs. Sometimes I would accompany these visitors to the tunnel for a briefing and photo opportunity. Usually they would also visit Panmunjom at the same time so they could be photographed with American soldiers overlooking the demarcation line. At times I felt more like a tour guide than an army officer. The Japanese attaché had a similarly heavy VIP load. At one time we had a contest to determine who had visited the tunnel the most times. Later I gave this duty to my assistant, though not before visiting the site over twenty times. The Japanese attaché had no assistant, and he continued to make these trips personally. He eventually became the champion tunnel visitor with over fifty trips, a record that probably still holds to this day.

My experiences under Ambassador Lilley reflected the myriad duties carried out by high-level embassy officials. My activities in the lead up to the 1987 presidential election and the 1988 Seoul Olympics were among the most important of my career with the U.S. government, ones that I recall with pride and satisfaction. Those involving the provision of services for visiting VIPs, however, are remembered with cynicism or humor, depending on my state of mind at any given time.

CHAPTER 12

Duty with Ambassador Gregg

illey's departure left a gap in the U.S. Embassy leadership for almost a year. Stan Brooks, who had been deputy ambassador under James Lilley, was placed in charge of the embassy until Donald Gregg could be confirmed by the U.S. Senate. Normally this process is fairly routine, but in Gregg's case it was not. Some Democratic senators believed that Gregg had been involved in some illegal activities involving support for the Nicaragua "contra" movement, and he also was accused of involvement in the "Irangate" scandal. Gregg had been in the CIA for many years, and following his retirement from that agency, he became Vice Pres. George Bush's national security advisor. His problems receiving timely confirmation were probably related more to politics than to any previous wrongdoing, but for whatever reason, he was unable to be confirmed for quite some time.

Gregg's nemesis in his Senate confirmation hearing was Sen. Alan Cranston of California. Cranston considered himself somewhat of an Asian expert and really gave the ambassador-designate a hard time. Gregg was not confirmed as ambassador until September 11, 1989, and then only by a 66-33 vote.[1] Because of his background and the fact that he had been the CIA station chief in Seoul on a previous assignment, Gregg's appointment was also controversial among some Koreans.[2] He turned out to be an excellent ambassador. Standing well over six feet tall and possessing a warm, open personality, he was very popular among Koreans by the time he left. I believe he was the best of the five ambassadors under whom I served, going all the way back to Ambassador Philip Habib in the early 1970s.

The initial opposition to Gregg by some Koreans was probably due to a misunderstanding of the role of the U.S. CIA. For many years, the Korean CIA had had both an international and domestic function and sometimes tended to concentrate on the domestic role to excess. In 1973, for instance, it kidnapped Kim Dae Jung in Japan and would have killed him had it not been for speedy U.S. intervention.[3] (Ironically Gregg was the U.S. CIA station chief at the time and was actively involved in resolving the case.) The KCIA was widely criticized or feared in Korea, even after the democratic reforms of 1987. Whatever its depredations abroad, the U.S. CIA has never had such a domestic role; in fact, it is prohibited by law from such activities. The great majority of CIA activities are routine and even boring. These involve study and analysis of economic trends, political analysis from such open sources as newspapers, electronic media, and other such analytical work. Most American CIA employees are little more than ordinary office workers, and they rarely experience anything more exciting than a bad traffic jam on their way home from work.

Anti-Americanism, Trade, and "Nordpolitik"

One of Ambassador Gregg's top priorities after arrival was how to counter the growing anti-Americanism in South Korea.[4] He believed that one of the reasons for this increasing problem was a failure to deal in a more direct manner with the confusion surrounding the American role during the 12/12 incident and its aftermath, particularly the American role in the Kwangju tragedy. It was not until June, 1989, that the U.S. government even made a formal statement on this period.

There were several reasons for this delay. First, until 1988, when the Korean National Assembly began its own investigation of these events and requested U.S. cooperation, there had been no formal request by the ROK government for an explanation of the U.S. role. Second, there was a natural bureaucratic reluctance in Washington to go back and address such matters, especially since over eight years had passed and the issue was not a domestic political concern in the United States. Also, most people did not associate anti-Americanism in Korea directly with these events. The most important reason, however, was that it would have been impossible to issue a comprehensive statement without embarrassing the Chun Doo Hwan government. Once Chun left office there was less resistance, and a fairly comprehensive statement was released in June, 1989.

Ambassador Gregg believed this statement had taken far too long to be issued. He had a strong affinity for the Korean people and felt a personal obligation to do anything possible to improve mutual understanding and stop the growing tide of anti-American feeling.

Gregg's deep affection for Koreans was largely a result of his CIA background. In addition to having been personally involved in negotiating the rescue of Kim Dae Jung in 1973, as a young man Gregg had secretly trained Korean agents for behind-the-lines intelligence work during the Korea War. I remember quite clearly his warm description of the young South Koreans who trained for these very dangerous missions. Ambassador Gregg's eyes would sometimes mist over when he spoke of those days, especially when he recalled that many of the brave men he trained never returned. I think all the ambassadors with whom I served enjoyed the company of their Korean friends and valued their friendship, but with Gregg it was a truly genuine and emotional relationship. He was a very pro-Korean ambassador, determined to take direct action whenever possible to counteract anti-Americanism.

As part of this effort, Gregg decided to pay an official visit to Kwangju. This would be the first such visit by an American ambassador since before the events of 1979–80. The Political Section was lukewarm on this idea, and the Public Affairs Office and the security officer were strongly opposed. They were especially concerned over the ambassador's safety. Special Assistant Jim McCullough (who had replaced John Stein in the summer of 1989) and I believed that there was certainly a security concern, but it was not so serious as to advise the ambassador not to go. No one in the embassy strongly supported the idea, however, since we did not believe such a trip would make much difference in countering hostility toward the United States.

Kim Dae Jung personally called Ambassador Gregg and advised him not to go to Kwangju. Because of this advice, Gregg again carefully considered canceling his trip but then decided to go ahead regardless of Kim's advice. Before departing, he put a personal handwritten note in his office safe stating that he was making the Kwangju trip against the advice of his staff and that, in the event he came to harm, he alone shouldered the blame. The trip went as scheduled, and I think can be considered a success, even though it did not significantly reduce anti-American sentiment.

A second incident occurred only three weeks after Gregg's September, 1989, arrival at the embassy.[5] This involved several radicals who entered the ambassador's compound early one morning and broke into his residence while he and his wife were sleeping. Being an old field-intelligence man, the ambassador had considered his escape plan previously, and he and his wife were able to slip out a rear bedroom window while the radicals were searching for them. The intruders occupied the residence for two hours or so, during which they destroyed the entire living area, including some personal items of sentimental value to the Greggs. They were finally evicted by embassy security personnel and arrested by the Korean police.

Some embassy staff, such as the security officer, were angry at what they considered lax security by the Korean police in this incident and thought was a late and ineffective response after the radicals had occupied the residence.

There was some sentiment for a strong protest to the ROK government over this matter. Ambassador Gregg immediately disagreed with this approach and instead directed the security officer to work in a calm and measured way with the Seoul police to review procedures in order to prevent another such incident. He then went on Korean television to actually praise the response of the police and stated that the break in was the work of only a small handful of Koreans and did not represent the actions or wishes of the Korean people at large. His quick and decisive action had an overall calming effect, and what might have been a major negative event became instead almost a positive one. In fact, I think that this incident actually helped ease anti-Americanism a little.

Another of Ambassador Gregg's priorities was to expand and balance trade with South Korea. Over the past generation we had developed a huge foreign-trade deficit, and there was a lot of pressure from Congress and the American business community to sell more American-made products internationally, including to Korea. In some respects, Korea was a victim of circumstances in this regard. The United States had for many years pursued a very generous trade policy with Japan, which had resulted in a serious trade deficit with that country. Now a deficit had emerged with Korea as well, and the U.S. Congress was not going to let that condition continue.[6] We in the embassy were under instructions to do everything possible to help balance trade with the ROK.

My office became quite involved in assisting American contractors, particularly defense contractors, understand the Korean market and its requirements. One of the things we always stressed to defense contractors was honesty and care in choosing agents. Some representatives had been rumored to be less than honest in their business dealings. This was especially the case with agents of some European companies that were competing against us on certain defense contracts and were involved in bribery. This finally caught up with them after the inauguration of Kim Young Sam as president of the ROK in 1993, and some of these people were arrested. As a result, the defense market in Korea is now considerably less subject to this type of illegal influence, and I think this will continue to work to the overall advantage of American companies, which are prohibited by U.S. law from these types of activities and are heavily punished if they break the law.

Some influential congressmen and senators from certain southern states were also pressuring us to sell more tobacco products in South Korea. The embassy staff and Ambassador Gregg all thought that these were unhealthy and a very poor choice of export. U.S. attempts to push tobacco products became a sort of renewed cause for anti-Americanism; as a result, we were really less than enthusiastic about this issue and did not push it very hard. Still, in July, 1988, the ROK government lifted longstanding restrictions on foreign tobacco imports, and during the first eleven months of 1989, U.S. companies sold 1.63 billion packs of cigarettes in South Korea.[7] Many Koreans believe that the embassy and U.S. government made tobacco a top priority, but in reality it was only one of many products we were to encourage Koreans to buy. Tobacco always had less importance to us than other items, including electronic components, aircraft and parts, industrial process controls, household items, medical equipment, and others. Fortunately my own responsibilities in this commercial area were primarily in the defense sector, and I was able to avoid the tobacco controversy.

There were some other issues between South Korea and the United States during this period that were misunderstood. An example was Roh Tae Woo's policy of improving relations with Communist countries, particularly the Soviet Union, sometimes referred to as "Nordpolitik." Some Koreans believed that the United States was opposed to these overtures because we wanted the ROK to remain solidly anti-Communist as an obstacle to Soviet expansionism, particularly in East Asia. This was not true. As a matter of fact, we encouraged these contacts and even worked behind the scenes to facilitate the success of Nordpolitik. An example was the meeting between Roh and Mikhail Gorbachev in San Francisco in June, 1990, which could never have been possible without American assistance. We worked to assist this improving relationship because we believed it was in the interest of both Korea and the United States, and a better relationship would tend to lessen active Soviet support for North Korea.[8]

Other Military Attachés

Most of my duties during this period were quite pleasant and not very controversial. The military attachés in South Korea had an association to which we all belonged, and we had monthly lunches together and a monthly dinner for the attachés and their wives. We saw each other frequently and socialized often, making many friends in the international community. Many of these officers were later promoted to general, a few reached the very senior ranks of their service, and one even became prime minister of his country.

The military attachés broke down into three basic groups. The first group was those who took their duties very seriously. These were generally officers from countries that had a close and important relationship with Korea, or some similar reason to pursue their duties diligently. This group included the American, the Japanese, and the German attachés. Members of the second group were interested in Korea, but their duties were often more representational than strictly professional, that is, the daily gathering of information and maintaining an in-depth understanding of the military situation. Unlike the first group, they had little or no Korean-language capability or background in the local history or culture. Most of the military attachés fell in this category, including those from Canada, Australia, Great Britain, Malaysia, and Italy, among others. The third group appeared to be in Korea for the primary reason of enjoying diplomatic life and parties. Some Latin American countries were in this group, and they hosted some very interesting affairs. Usually their offices did not open until about 11:00 A.M. and then closed early in the afternoon. They would then gather for a late supper, followed by dancing and other party activities until very late in the evening. I envied their social life, but soon found that it was impossible to keep such a schedule and still function effectively the next day. All in all, the attaché group was a lot of fun, and we enjoyed our association with each other immensely.

Other Activities

We also were able to play some golf during this tour, especially with my Korean military friends. From time to time, however, the Roh government would decide that golf was not appropriate for senior military officers or other government officials.

I had been in the habit of playing about once a month with a certain General Kang, who was crazy about the sport. We had established a golf date well in advance, but between then and the actual tee time, there was some economic downturn or other minicrisis, and the Roh government was discouraging golf participation. When I arrived at the golf club, I did not even recognize my good friend Kang. He was almost in a state of total disguise, wearing sunglasses with a hat pulled down on his face and a large overcoat, even though it was very warm. He also had used a friend's automobile to drive himself to the club so his own license plate would not be seen in the parking lot. Such were the measures that some would go to in order to enjoy a round of golf!

I also participated occasionally in traditional Korean *kisaeng* parties with some generals and other Korean friends from the business community. The normal practice was for these events to be officially hosted by a military officer, but the actual bill was usually paid by one of the businessmen, who enjoyed a much higher salary. I always enjoyed these events and learned several Korean songs in order to participate more actively. All Koreans seem to have beautiful voices, but most Americans sound like frogs when they sing. With a little practice, however, I became above average in talent among my friends.

One requirement of my job was to occasionally escort Korean VIPs when they would visit the United States on official business. This included such people as the ROK minister of defense, army chief of staff, and sometimes the Korea DIA director. One such trip occurred in conjunction with the 1989 Security Consultative Meeting, which was hosted by Secretary of Defense Dick Cheney in Washington. My assignment was to escort Korean Defense Minister Lee Sang Hoon.

If ordinary Korean and American citizens realized exactly how these VIP trips are structured and conducted on both sides, I think they would have every reason to be frustrated about the way their tax dollars are spent. In this case, it was truly a first-class trip. We began in Los Angeles, but the only real business conducted there was a short visit on the second day to the facilities of a major American defense company; most of the time was spent visiting with Minister Lee and his wife's relatives and playing golf. The third day we flew on our private jet, flown and staffed by U.S. Air Force personnel, to Seattle, where we visited the Boeing Company, then we flew to nearby Fort Lewis, Washington, for some briefings and to observe military training. After that we traveled to Colorado Springs for a tour of the North American Air Defense headquarters; then we flew to the resort area of Williamsburg, Virginia, for more golf, some historical tours, and a visit to a U.S. nuclear submarine. This was about a five-day taxpayer-financed vacation followed by the three-day security consultative meeting in Washington.

Even the "business" portion of this and similar trips was pretty relaxed, with cocktail parties and receptions each evening and fancy luncheons hosted each day. Most of the so-called business conducted was routine in nature and could easily have been accomplished without the trouble and expense of an international meeting.[9] Each side brought thirty or forty senior aides, generals, and their staff members, far more than were needed to transact the relatively simple government business on the agenda.

The Cost-Sharing Issue

One important item on which I was deeply involved during this period was cost sharing, which concerned what portion of the costs of maintaining U.S. forces in Korea should be paid by the ROK government. As the major military power in the world, the United States maintains forces all over the globe. A number of multilateral and bilateral agreements determine how and by whom the costs of maintaining those forces are paid. When the ROK was struggling to recover from the Korean War and was still developing its economy, the United States assumed 100 percent of these costs. As the Cold War wound down in the late 1980s and the U.S. budget deficit skyrocketed, pressure increased from Washington to negotiate agreements similar to others around the world, with Korea paying some portion of these expenses.

These negotiations were often protracted. Since both countries believed that the presence of American forces in Korea was in the long-term interests of both South Korea and the United States, it was difficult to reach an exact formula upon which each side could agree. The fact that the ROK provided without charge land and facilities for the use of U.S. forces added complications in the effort to calculate each other's contributions. So did the fact that U.S. soldiers enjoyed amenities well beyond those provided by the ROK for its troops. Eventually we devised a sort of graduated scale whereby Korea would pay an increasing portion of American costs, particularly those associated with the many Korean employees and contractors of U.S. Forces Korea. It was an example of give and take by both sides on an issue that, given the new openness of South Korean politics and pressures from the U.S. Congress to reduce the American troop presence, might have become a source of friction.

The Yongsan Golf Course

Another issue was the future of the Yongsan Golf Course. USFK had occupied the Yongsan area since the end of World War II and over the years had built a small golf course on the south end of the post. At the time this facility was constructed, it was almost in the countryside, but with the rapid growth of Seoul to the south, it had become very centrally located. The existence of this golf course in the center of the Seoul metropolitan area was a sensitive political issue, especially in the now democratic ROK. Many Korean officials and others wanted the property returned to the government for use as a park.

This was a real point of contention between USFK and the embassy. USFK wanted to retain the golf course as a recreation facility for its soldiers, but the embassy wanted to turn it over as soon as possible to the Korean government. This also became a personal issue between Ambassador Lilley and Gen. Louis Menetrey, especially after Lilley, without Menetrey's knowledge, sent a personal message to both the secretary of state and secretary of defense arguing that the golf course should be returned as soon as possible. After the arrival of Ambassador Gregg, the relationship between USFK and the embassy improved, but for a while the atmosphere was somewhat tense.

Just as things seemed to be moving smoothly toward resolution of this issue with the ROK, my wife, Jody, an avid golfer, unexpectedly seized the initiative. In February, 1990, Secretary of Defense Cheney visited Seoul.[10] As was normal in such high-level visits, the most senior defense officials on both sides, along with senior diplomatic representatives and a host of generals and other bigwigs, were involved.

Most of the formal meetings went smoothly, for the staffs had worked out the details much earlier. The golf course issue, it had been previously agreed, would not be raised because of its controversial nature. The plan, at least from the embassy's point of view, was to present the handover of the golf course as a *fait accompli* at the end of the next year's security consultative meeting.

Unfortunately no one had consulted my wife on the matter. She had been elected president of the Yongsan Ladies Golf Association the previous year and was so popular with the golfing ladies that she was elected to an unprecedented second term. By a quirk of fate, and by virtue of being the wife of the senior military officer in the embassy, she was also chosen as Secretary of Defense Cheney's dinner partner for the formal banquet hosted in his honor. I sat next to the secretary's wife, Lynn, a most distinguished person in her own right and an engaging and lively dinner partner.

What government officials had vigorously worked for weeks to keep off the secretary's agenda was soon raised at dinner by Jody. She explained to Secretary Cheney the lack of normal recreational options afforded U.S. military families in South Korea and the importance of the golf course as an outlet in a strange and unfamiliar country. She made an impassioned plea that the secretary consider the morale and welfare of military families serving in Korea as well as the strategic issues that were the normal fare of such high-level meetings. Cheney listened attentively and made some notes on his speech text, which he had been reviewing under the table during dinner. During his formal speech after dinner, he inserted remarks emphasizing the importance of the morale and welfare issues Jody had raised. The American secretary of defense had now weighed in on the side of our troops. So much for carefully laid staff work and diplomacy.

The U.S. Army finally gave up the golf course in November, 1992, but then only after the Korean government built a replacement course in the Songnam area not far from Seoul.

The F-16–F/A-18 and P3C-Atlantique Competitions

As indicated previously, part of my job as defense attaché was to assist U.S. business interests, especially defense-related contractors, in their efforts to compete successfully for contracts in South Korea. This part of my job became even more important in the latter part of 1989 and early 1990, when American companies were in some fierce competition over two big contracts.

The first of these contracts involved the ROK Air Force's new-generation fighter aircraft, which we referred to as the KFP (Korea Fighter Program). The two competitors were major American companies, with General Dynamics (later Lockheed) encouraging the Korean government to buy the F-16 and McDonnell Douglas marketing the F/A-18. The F-16 was already in the ROK Air Force inventory and had some advantages in terms of logistical support and the fact that the ROKAF already had trained pilots and crews. Also, the F-16 was less expensive. As a result, General Dynamics was originally very confident that it would win the contract. McDonnell Douglas was considered a big underdog, but it had a good marketing team and was able to win support for its airplane from the ROKAF on the basis of superior performance, a higher level of technology transfer, and the fact that the F/A-18 had two engines, which most pilots preferred for safety reasons.

Because there were two American companies competing, embassy personnel were under strict instructions to be completely impartial. Behind the scenes, however, there was a lot of maneuvering going on by both companies to make it appear that they had the support of the U.S. government. This was compounded by the fact that the U.S. Air Force strongly desired the F-16 to be chosen, while the U.S. Navy, which operates the F/A-18, wanted Korea to choose that plane. Each of the corporations hired big-name lobbyists, retired generals, and sent briefing teams to Korea to try to convince the government to buy their airplane. The U.S. Air Force and U.S. Navy were also working aggressively in private to encourage the selection of their favorite fighter. It was a tough competition, but MND eventually sided with the ROKAF and chose the F/A-18.

After the official announcement that the F/A-18 had been chosen, the F-16 proponents began to lobby strongly to the Blue House to have the decision overruled. Each side made charges against the other, accusing one another of payoffs and similar dirty tricks. Eventually the F/A-18 decision was overturned and the F-16 selected.[11] Despite pressure from both the F-16 and F/A-18 companies, I was happy to be able to avoid any direct involvement in this controversy.

The second defense program in which we had a major interest was the ROK Navy's antisubmarine-aircraft program. The American candidate was the P3C, a very capable aircraft with which the U.S. Navy had had great success. The P3C was manufactured by Lockheed, and the competition was a French aircraft called the Atlantique. The P3C was a superior aircraft from an operational standpoint and had a far more technically sophisticated capability. There were also logistical and operational advantages because the P3C could be used in combined operations with U.S. Navy forces, a serious consideration since the French, unlike the Americans, did not actively exercise their forces near the Korean peninsula. The French aircraft had a slightly lower price, however, so it was a close competition.

Ambassador Gregg took a major role in promoting the P3C. Unlike the F-16–F/A-18 competition, which involved two American companies, this time there was only a single U.S. company involved. Our strategy was to provide all the information requested by the Koreans to emphasize that this was an important contract to the American side but to avoid pressuring our Korean allies into the sale. Both Ambassador Gregg and I felt that a reasonably low-key approach would be successful, and that was the strategy we pursued.

On the day that the decision was scheduled to be announced, the French, who had put enormous pressure on South Korea to buy the Atlantique, were certain they had won. The French defense minister came to Seoul and scheduled a big party in anticipation of victory. That afternoon, the ROK government announced the selection of the American P3C. The French minister was so angry that he refused to attend his own reception, and he left Seoul the next day, abruptly canceling several appointments.

Since then there have been several investigations and even some arrests in conjunction with other defense plans and programs. As someone who has observed these programs and been involved in the details of these competitions, I think this is a healthy sign. A clean and honest acquisition program is essential to the overall security of the country and is necessary to ensure the support and confidence of the Korean people. My experience indicates that the continuation and successful completion of the defense-improvement program is necessary and important, and I hope that those who abuse their position of responsibility will continue to be exposed and punished.

Retirement from the Army

In early January, 1990, I was faced with a difficult decision. My assignment as defense attaché was scheduled to end that summer, and the most likely next assignment was back to Washington to either a high-level staff job in the Pentagon or as East Asia bureau chief at the DIA. Neither of these jobs really appealed to me, and I was anxious to try my hand at something different. I had never had the burning ambition to be a general and felt as if I had already accomplished everything in the army that I wanted; I had enjoyed an exciting and rewarding military career. After discussing it with my family, we decided that I would voluntarily retire from the service that summer. This was not an easy decision since, including my cadet years, I had worn an army uniform for thirty-one years. But all good things must come to an end eventually.

The days leading up to my retirement were busy and passed quickly. It seemed as if all my friends wanted to provide a farewell party, and I will remember those times fondly. There were retirement and award ceremonies at the embassy, hosted by Ambassador Gregg, and also at the Pentagon after we returned to Washington. There was also an award ceremony at the South Korean Embassy in Washington a few weeks later—all in all, I left active military service with a great deal of satisfaction and contentment.

CHAPTER 13

Journey to North Korea

n the spring of 1991, I received a telephone call from Gen. Richard Stilwell, who was commander of U.S. Forces Korea from 1974 to 1976. General Stilwell had been a particularly distinguished officer and was highly respected on both the Korean and American sides. Following his retirement from the U.S. Army, he had been a consultant to several companies and was also appointed to a high civilian-government position during the Reagan administration. Throughout these years, Stilwell had maintained his close ties to Korea and was active in several organizations that focused on Korean politics, security, and military affairs.

General Stilwell said in our conversation that he expected to make a trip to Pyongyang, North Korea, in the middle of June and requested that I accompany him. This came as quite a surprise since it was difficult for me to imagine the former commander of USFK visiting North Korea. Although I had some concerns, I had great respect for General Stilwell and therefore agreed to his request.

In the beginning, this trip was considered a secret since the United States and North Korea (officially the Democratic People's Republic of Korea) had never previously had contact such as this. The State Department was concerned that news of our mission would leak out and that South Korea would object. Rather than try to keep it a secret, however, General Stilwell suggested that we instead inform our ROK allies in advance about all the details and debrief them fully on return. This was the approach that was eventually adopted, and our trip was made with the full knowledge of both the American and South Korean governments.

The purpose of our visit was to discuss with senior North Korean officials issues of mutual concern related to security on the Korean peninsula. There would be a two-day formal conference and meetings with the defense and foreign ministers and possibly even Kim Il Sung, the North Korean leader. Our trip was under the banner of the International Security Council (ISC), a Washington-based group whose worldwide membership includes many distinguished Americans and foreigners. General Stilwell headed the delegation, which also included Dr. Joseph Churba, the president of the ISC; Generals Raymond G. Davis and Robert Bazley, retired four-star generals of the Marine Corps and the U.S. Air Force respectively; Rear Adm. James Nance (ret.), former deputy assistant to the president for national security affairs; Sol Sanders, a distinguished journalist; Professors William R. Van Cleave and A. James Gregor, two respected professors of political science; and myself. It would be the first direct contact with North Korea by such a high-level group since the Korean War, and we were eagerly anticipating this trip as the date grew near.

Because the United States and North Korea had no official diplomatic relations, our trip was considered to be an unofficial visit by private citizens. Despite this nonofficial status, we were given extensive briefings in Washington about current policy and were well prepared before leaving. At one point we were even personally briefed by Assistant Secretary of State for East Asia Richard Solomon. So even though our official status was lacking, we were expected to observe U.S. policy guidelines and to give an extensive report to all appropriate government agencies upon our return from Pyongyang.

We departed from New York, and while waiting in the VIP room at Kennedy International Airport, we were visited by Mr. Ho Jung, the number-two man in the North Korean United Nations delegation. I had met Ho before and considered him to be a clever man and a polished "barbarian handler," as we called those officials whose primary duty was to liaison with the Americans and other foreigners. He was accompanied by a second North Korean since DPRK citizens never went anywhere alone. Officially the North Koreans claimed they went everywhere in pairs to avoid being kidnapped or for some similar security reason, but actually it was probably also to prevent the defection of one of their diplomats.

Since I had known Ho Jung previously, I introduced him to General Stilwell. Stilwell was concerned about both the agenda and the level of persons that we would meet, and he discussed these matters with Ho. At the time I thought Stilwell was going to refuse to travel any further; in fact at one point he seemed determined to return to Washington. Finally he was persuaded otherwise, and we boarded the plane for Beijing. This was only the beginning of several problems between Stilwell and the North Koreans.

The one-day stopover in Beijing was for the purpose of changing planes and obtaining visas. Since the United States had no diplomatic relations with North Korea, we had to receive our entry visa from the DPRK Embassy in Beijing. These were supposed to be issued at 9:00 A.M., and we would then fly to Pyongyang two hours later aboard a North Korean commercial airplane. Unfortunately, when our administrative officer arrived at the embassy, there was no one available to issue our visas. It seemed that we had arrived at the same time they were closed for ideological training and study of the *Juche* idea, the North Korean doctrine or "self-reliance" developed by Pres. Kim Il Sung. After about two hours they had apparently had enough training for the day, and our visas were subsequently issued. We left for the Beijing airport soon thereafter.

Our flight to Pyongyang was aboard a "Chosun Minhang" Russian-built aircraft, which could be configured for either passenger or cargo transport and was reasonably comfortable. We flew a somewhat circuitous route, from Beijing over northeastern China and Manchuria and then on a line roughly from Sinuiju to Pyongyang.

The weather was clear and sunny, and I was able to get an excellent view of the North Korean countryside. As I looked down, I could not help but be reminded of my first arrival in the ROK almost thirty years previously. The road networks were mostly dirt, with very limited traffic, and only an occasional dark green military truck was visible as we flew over. I was struck by how underdeveloped the countryside appeared to be and by the lack of any traffic or commercial activity. The difference between this sight and the hustle and bustle of the road networks in the South was like night and day. Even though we were well aware of the vast economic difference between North and South Korea, it was still a shock to actually see this almost total absence of activity.

Landing at Pyongyang, we were met with a large picture of the "Great Leader" (Kim Il Sung) and by our North Korean hosts for the week. The senior man was Song Ho Gyong, president of the DPRK's Institute for Disarmament and Peace. Others with whom we would spend the next few days included Maj. Gen. Kim Yong Chol of the Korean People's Army; Kim Byong Hong, vice president of the Institute for Disarmament and Peace; and Li Hyong Chol, director of the same institute. This was the same group that had participated in some of the North-South discussions both preceding and following our trip. As we grew more familiar with these individuals, it became clear that General Kim was a person of some special authority.

City of Pyongyang

I found Pyongyang to be an interesting place. It had wide boulevards, large and impressive government buildings, and many monuments (usually dedicated to the Great Leader) throughout the city. It reminded me a little of Washington, but only in its similarity as a national capital with many government buildings. There was a very low population density, for the government forbade most ordinary citizens from living in the city. It was clean and did not appear to suffer from air pollution. It was also the most lifeless and sterile place I think I have ever visited.

Our hotel was the Koryo Hotel, located near the Pyongyang Railroad Station in the Central District of the city. The hotel was an impressive structure from the outside, with twin towers rising about thirty stories on each side. Although the hotel had a sizeable capacity, it was certainly not busy. Each morning at breakfast I counted the guests, and after several days determined that there were probably no more than forty people staying in the entire hotel. There were no other guests on my floor, and the same was true for several of the rest of us. Only on my last night in Pyongyang did other guests arrive on my floor—a middle-aged Korean American couple who had been visiting relatives near Haeju.

My room was actually a small suite and was quite comfortable, although the design was far from modern. There were three rooms: one for sleeping; one for work, which included a large and handsome wooden desk; and a living room area with a small table and television. Next to the bed were two telephones, one of these was connected to the hotel operator, and the other appeared to be a listening device. As a former intelligence officer, I was amused at this old-fashioned method of monitoring the room. It reminded me of some old World War II spy movie.

The room also had a minibar in the refrigerator that was stocked with snacks and drinks. Each day a three-person team of "minibar inspectors" comprised of two women and one male supervisor would inspect and completely inventory the contents. The first woman would physically check each item and announce its condition as satisfactory, then the second woman would double check each item and check it off the written inventory. The man's job appeared to be to observe the entire operation. It was never clear why this relatively simple task required three people, but it may have been indicative of a pilferage problem or simply an overabundance of hotel employees with nothing to do. At any rate, it was interesting to watch this process, which occurred like clockwork each day.

At the time, and I think it is even more so today, Pyongyang was suffering from a serious power shortage. Few of the electrically powered facilities in the hotel were operating, including the escalator in the center of the lobby. Only a minimum of lights were on, and after dark there were only a few scattered street lamps and no activity to speak of. Pyongyang after dark was truly a ghost town. On one occasion I purposely left a single small light burning in my room. I then left briefly and returned. In my absence someone had entered the room and switched off the light, even though I had been gone less than five minutes. Few of the electrically driven transportation systems appeared to be running on a regular basis—most people walked to their destinations or waited in line for public transportation. There were no taxis, no bicycles, and only a few small buses, which appeared to be operated for the benefit of special groups rather than as part of the public transportation network.

On our first night in Pyongyang, I accompanied another member of our group to a small bar in the basement of the Koryo Hotel. At this bar, which was only for foreigners, were about ten people, all men, from a variety of countries. The foreign community in Pyongyang was quite small, so when we entered we were immediately recognized as newcomers. One of the people next to me, a Frenchman, introduced himself and asked what country we were from. I replied that we were Americans. At this time, from a few seats away, I heard a loud voice say in Korean, "American rascal! Crush him! We will crush American Imperialism!"

This voice came from a husky-looking North Korean wearing his Kim Il Sung button. He was obviously part of the security apparatus assigned to monitor activities and conversations at the several small bars in central Pyongyang serving the foreign community. I paused for a moment and then responded in an equally loud voice and also in Korean, "Why would you want to crush me?" He was surprised and taken aback that I understood Korean, and he appeared embarrassed. Later we had a drink together and a good laugh. It turned out that this fellow had once visited New York, of which he was very proud, since North Koreans were not allowed to travel overseas under normal circumstances. At any rate, we ended the evening on a friendly basis, and thankfully I was not "crushed."

I had an acquaintance in Pyongyang who had been there for sometime and knew the city well. At one time this individual had been assigned to the Czech-Polish contingent on the Neutral Nations Supervisory Commission, which was at a small camp near Kaesong. We had become acquainted at that time, and now he was the Czech ambassador in Pyongyang. On the second day of our visit, he hosted a private luncheon for General Stilwell and myself, and that evening he volunteered to take me around town.

Nightlife in Pyongyang was almost nonexistent, but there were a few small bars similar to the one in the hotel. These establishments, I was told, as well as two or three small restaurants in the same area, were controlled by expatriate Japanese. They appeared to be private enterprises, which were allowed to operate as long as the proprietors catered only to foreigners and made a suitable "donation" to Kim Il Sung. We went to two of these, accompanied by a friend of the Czech ambassador, a Russian who had been in Pyongyang for six years working as a "press attaché" for the Soviet Embassy. Since at the time the local Pyongyang *Pravda* office had already closed, and since six years is a very long time for a press attaché to stay in one place, I assumed this man was in reality the KGB chief. At any rate, he was very helpful, knowledgeable, and a good source of information as to the current situation and events in the area. Some people may think it strange that a Soviet KGB agent and a former American military-intelligence officer would be openly discussing such matters of mutual interest in a bar in Pyongyang, but by June, 1991, the Cold War was over and it was not unusual for such cooperation to take place, especially in relation to North Korea, a country with few remaining friends.

Television in the North, as with the other electronic and print media, was essentially just another forum for propaganda. Every program, even the "entertainment" shows, had a political or nationalistic message. News clips always had a political slant and usually featured as the highlight some visiting dignitary paying a call on Kim Il Sung. During our visit, the president of the Maldives was visiting Pyongyang, and there was news footage of him paying a visit to Kim Il Sung and later inspecting some vegetables at a collective farm. The footage of the Great Leader I found to be very interesting— although he seemed to walk slowly with the short "shuffle-step" of an older man, he seemed very alert. The growth on his neck was usually shielded by the camera angle, but from later film that I viewed, this growth was really enormous, much larger than I had expected.

People often ask about food shortages in North Korea. As a VIP group, we were guests of the state and treated well, but my impression was that, even in the capital city, there were some food shortages. Once while walking down a side street a short distance from the hotel, I came upon an older woman who was displaying some very poor-quality fruit, apparently for sale, on a blanket. As I stopped to talk to her, a security man suddenly appeared and ordered her to leave the area immediately. This was the only fresh produce I saw available for purchase, although there must have been some sort of market somewhere in the area.

Much of the food served to our group was processed food rather than fresh, and it was of modest quality. The menu at the hotel dining room was extensive, but most of the listed items were unavailable. Even at our VIP-type banquets, of which there were several, the food was adequate but not exceptional, comparable to a slightly below-average restaurant in Seoul. I am not complaining, for our North Korean hosts probably did as well as they could with what resources were available. My impression, however, was that there was likely a serious problem in the North, particularly in the countryside, in both the quantity and quality of available food.[1]

I also visited a department store in Pyongyang near the train station. It was adequately stocked, though with goods few Westerners would want to buy. I visited this store twice, but neither time was there any sales activity or customers around. At one time I attempted to buy a fountain pen, but the clerk did not have a key to the display case, and her supervisor could not locate the key either. I got the impression that I might have been their only customer that day, or maybe even that year.

For most of the time, we were confined to Pyongyang; however, one morning we were permitted a field trip to visit a large dam project. This was an interesting drive along part of the Taedong River, which empties into the Yellow Sea west of Pyongyang, and along the outskirts of the city of Nampo. The road was paved and wide but poorly engineered, and therefore it tended to be bumpy. We were given a briefing and a short tour of the "Western Barrage" project and then returned to Pyongyang. Although we were not permitted to spend much time outside the capital, General Stilwell was successful in arranging a visit to Sariwon. He had asked repeatedly to be allowed to make a sentimental visit to Kaesong, near the armistice line and where he had spent time during the Korean War, but the North Koreans refused.

Stilwell also wanted to see the Pyongyang subway, which we visited, accompanied by a guide. The subway is very deep and perhaps is designed to serve as a civil-defense shelter, for the waiting platforms are very wide, roomy, and often decorated with colorful ceramic mosaics or pictures. Like so many other things in Pyongyang, however, it seemed to serve more as a monument to Kim Il Sung than as an effective transportation system. As far as I could determine, there were only two main lines, so it appeared that a sizeable portion of the city was without direct subway access. After riding the subway for a few minutes, it began to fill with people. Soon a woman with a small child entered the car, but there was no seat available. As was the American custom, Stilwell offered his seat to the woman, who seemed quite surprised and initially refused to take it. Eventually she sat down after the general insisted. All of the subway riders were surprised at this action by this strange American visitor, and I could not help but wonder how much more surprised they would have been if they had known his identity and background.

We were, by coincidence, in Pyongyang at the same time that the North Koreans were celebrating "anti-American month." As a result, there were many mass parades and demonstrations, particularly by youth groups. As we exited the subway near the location of Pyongyang's famous "Arch of Triumph," some of these "mass games" were underway, with large formations of young North Koreans shouting pro–Kim Il Sung and anti-American slogans. Stilwell was fascinated by the spectacle and refused to leave even when our very nervous guide insisted. Again, I wondered at the irony of the former USFK commander observing anti-American mass rallies in a hostile capital city.

If there were any disappointments during this trip, it was the inability to spend much time in the countryside or to have a chance to meet many ordinary North Korean citizens. The DPRK authorities did not encourage contact between their citizens and foreigners, and they were especially careful about restricting these contacts once our hosts learned that I could understand Korean. Hopefully some day this situation will change and direct contacts between North Korean citizens and outsiders will be expanded. My impression is, however, that the present North Korean government greatly fears such open contact, for once the truth about living standards and other characteristics of the outside world are well known, it will cause a lot of problems in the North due to the rising expectations of their own citizens.

Meetings with North Korean Leaders

General Kim Kwan Jin

Soon after our arrival in Pyongyang, we met with the DPRK acting defense minister, Gen. Kim Kwan Jin. Kim and General Stilwell sat side by side as the two senior members, with the rest of us seated along each side. Kim initiated the conversation by welcoming us to Pyongyang and assuring us that it was the policy of his government to encourage contacts between Americans and North Koreans. He noted that it would have been better if we had come while still on active duty, which we interpreted as underscoring the desire for "official" contacts with the United States. Stilwell replied that several of our delegation had indeed visited North Korea previously while on active duty but had found it to be a bit inhospitable since it was during the Korean War.

Kim then launched into a lengthy review of North Korea's policy on various issues, including reunification, relations with the United States, and defense matters.[2] He spoke of the need for the reunification of the Korean peninsula, though only as a confederation on North Korea's terms. He said that detente and collaboration should replace confrontation but then quickly added that this could occur only if the United States changed its policies. North Korea, he emphasized, must be treated as an equal, not as a nation that could be dictated to.

Surprisingly, Kim acknowledged that military expenditures were a burden on the DPRK economy. He said that there had been a recent 100,000-man reduction in the North's armed forces and that another 150,000 were dedicated almost entirely to civil-works projects. As expected, he attacked the annual U.S.-ROK military exercise Team Spirit, which he blamed for disrupting the North-South dialogue. For example, Kim said, cancellation of the 1991 exercise had been requested by the DPRK as a condition for North Korean participation in the previously scheduled prime ministers' session. The ROK had been willing to cancel, he alleged inaccurately, but the United States refused and thus was responsible for the suspension of these high-level talks.

Stilwell reminded Kim that he personally had initiated the Team Spirit exercises in 1976 and therefore was very familiar with the scope and purpose of the exercise. The sole purpose of Team Spirit was to assure the U.S. capability to carry out its commitment to help defend against any further aggression from the North, and it was in no way provocative. Kim replied that the DPRK had not objected to Team Spirit when it was of smaller scale, but now it had become a "reinforcement" exercise involving 200,000 U.S. troops.

I was surprised that the senior military officer in North Korea was so unfamiliar with the actual facts concerning Team Spirit. For example, the 1991 exercise involved only about 16,000 U.S. troops, far less than the 200,000 Kim stated. Also, it was impossible for the United States to continue this exercise in 1991 or any other year without the cooperation and support of the ROK, which provided the bulk of the forces and internal support.[3] This was the first of several indications we received that the North Korean leadership was not particularly well informed about some important matters.

Foreign Minister Kim Yong Nam

If the meeting with Kim Kwan Jin had been less than satisfactory, our next meeting, which was with Foreign Minister Kim Yong Nam, was even more so. The meeting was held in the National Assembly building, a huge and imposing structure that appeared to be quite empty. After a short tour of the facility, of which the North Koreans seemed quite proud, we entered a large conference room to meet Kim Yong Nam.

Within Pyongyang's small diplomatic community, Kim had a reputation for extended tirades and for his skill in leaving Western visitors with the worst possible impression of his country. After a two-hour meeting, our delegation was convinced that this reputation was well deserved.

The foreign minister began by speculating that the presence of this American delegation in Pyongyang might indicate a partial U.S. reevaluation of its Korean policy, which historically discouraged its citizens from visiting the DPRK. He called for increased contacts but then immediately began to complain that there had been no change in U.S. policies, which refused to recognize realities, blocked peaceful reunification, and slandered North Korea.

Kim said that his country had long sought to establish closer contact and better relations with the United States and listed several examples. In 1983, he recalled, the DPRK National Assembly wrote to the U.S. Congress in this regard. A year later North Korea proposed the idea of three-way talks between North and South Korea and the United States. Although the political counselors of the United States and North Korean embassies in Beijing meet regularly and other avenues of communication were available, Kim noted, the United States had yet to respond to the North Korean proposals. He charged that the United States was "timid, narrow-minded, and indecisive"—later he added "small-hearted" and "feeble-minded." I could see General Stilwell's facial muscles tighten in reaction to this name calling, but he maintained his calm and composure.

To grasp North Korean reality, Kim said, it was necessary to understand the nature of the DPRK, the issue of reunification, and the Korean policies of both the United States and Japan. He emphasized his country's total independence, its unflagging devotion to *Juche* as the very soul of North Korea, and its rejection of all other foreign philosophies. North Korea, Kim insisted, was the equal of all other states, including the great powers; there could never be dominant and subordinate states.

Following this lecture on the superiority of the *Juche* idea, Kim turned to the subject of reunification. Reunification, he continued, was important because it would remove a potential cause of war and reunite a divided nation. Under the North Korean confederation plan, a unified Korea could initially incorporate the two competing systems, but eventually these systems would become complementary. He summarily dismissed all alternative South Korean proposals, instead calling for the concept of one nation and one state but two systems and two governments. The confederation would have one national assembly and an executive committee in which North and South Koreans would be represented on equal footing with representatives of overseas Koreans. The chairmanship would rotate annually between North and South. Kim suggested the replacement of the armistice with an agreement between the two Koreas that would convert the DMZ into a temporary boundary, pending reunification.

The foreign minister said North Korea was closely monitoring American policy through the news media and occasional visits to the United States. He criticized the "heavy-handed" policy of the United States, which attached preconditions to an improvement in relations. He also charged that Japan wanted to improve relations with the DPRK but that the United States and South Korea were blocking this. Kim further stated, without much evidence, that Japan was demanding international inspection of North Korea's nuclear facilities as a precondition to improved relations because it wished once more to become a military power, specifically a nuclear power, and replace the United States as the dominant force in Asia. After almost one and a half hours of nonstop lecturing, Kim finally stopped talking.

Responding in part to Kim's extended admonition, General Stilwell noted that our delegation had come to Pyongyang with the understanding that North Korea wanted an open and frank dialogue. We assumed, he said, that North Korea's deteriorating economy, the loss of its credit rating, and its heavy defense burden might be influencing the country to adopt more flexible policies. Based on our meetings thus far, however, Stilwell said we had yet to detect any change. Like North Korea, the United States had conditions for an improvement in bilateral relations, including renunciation of terrorism, adherence to the nuclear safeguards agreement, and a more responsible policy regarding the export of weapons (for example, intermediate-range missiles to the Middle East). As for U.S. policy toward the Korean peninsula, Stilwell said that our steady policy did not reflect a lack of courage but caution and prudence because the well being of seventy million Koreans was at stake.

General Stilwell then made a surprise offer to the North Koreans. He offered to provide up to one hundred scholarships for North Korean students to study at colleges and universities in the United States. The DPRK government would choose the students, he said, and the subjects they would study. Kim was initially taken aback by this proposal, which was totally unexpected, and did not respond. Toward the end of the meeting, Stilwell repeated the offer, and by now Kim had recovered sufficiently to reject it as being "inappropriate."

The Conference on Korea Security

If the meetings with the senior DPRK leadership had been less than satisfactory, any hopes that the actual conference would produce better results were quickly dashed. Despite an earlier agreement on a specific agenda, the North Koreans began by putting forward a printed version of their own agenda and then proceeded to follow it for the duration of the two-day conference. The result was that we were sometimes talking about different issues. For example, the North Koreans insisted on discussing their own formula for reunification, but we believed that this was basically an issue between the ROK and DPRK and inappropriate for us to discuss. Anyhow, the conference centered around three topics: arms control on the Korean peninsula, U.S.–North Korean relations, and nuclear energy and weapons.

Arms Control

General Stilwell opened the formal conference on the subject of arms control.[4] He emphasized that the principal cause of tension on the Korean peninsula was the large concentration of military forces on both sides of the Demilitarized Zone. North Korean forces, in particular, were larger than those of the ROK, were structured for an offensive capability, and were deployed to attack with little or no warning.

In an effort to find a successful precedent for arms control, Stilwell noted that negotiations for the reduction of arms in Europe had been a long and difficult process. During the first ten years of the talks, little was achieved because the negotiators were unable to agree on a common set of facts. Only after the Soviet Union agreed to provide accurate data on the size and capabilities of its armed forces was progress achieved. Stilwell said the same holds true for future negotiations on the peninsula, noting that North Korea refused to provide information on the strength and equipment of its armed forces and denied the accuracy of information published by a variety of reputable sources, which estimated the North Korean Army at over one million men. He asked that the DPRK be more open during the conference and said he was willing to provide them with his own estimates of North Korean forces. Without agreement on the military strength of either nation, there could be no real confidence that the two sides were negotiating in good faith.

From the beginning of their answering statement, it was clear that the North Korean side was more interested in presenting its own views than in exploring any new solutions. Speaking for the DPRK, Maj. Gen. Kim Yong Chul stated the often-repeated position that a declaration of nonaggression between North and South Korea was a prerequisite for arms reduction. North Korea first proposed such a declaration in 1984, he said, that called for mutual recognition and respect, the peaceful resolution of disputes, an end to the propaganda war, effective military confidence building, and a phased reduction of arms. A nonaggression declaration would begin to dispel mistrust and build confidence, Kim argued. Once such a declaration was adopted, exchange of information on military exercises and military strength would be possible. He called further for a separate U.S.–North Korean peace treaty.

General Kim dismissed the comparison to negotiations on arms reduction in Europe, arguing that such comparisons were not relevant to the Korean situation. The best formula for building mutual confidence, he said, was a declaration of nonaggression. I then asked Kim whether the free movement of ideas and people would not contribute to the reduction of tension. He replied somewhat reluctantly that it would be helpful, but that could only occur once the military confrontation had been reduced.

Following some more give and take, our group was asked to endorse the DPRK proposal for a North-South declaration of nonaggression. Both Generals Davis and Bazley, who had little experience concerning Communist negotiating and propaganda techniques, indicated that they would consider endorsing such a plan. General Stilwell quickly intervened, however, and would have nothing of it. He pointed out that he was not familiar with the specific language or the negotiating history that surrounded the proposal, and indeed, nonaggression with respect to all other states would be an explicit commitment assumed when the two states enter the United Nations. What was important, he said, was the mutual undertakings and actions that gave real meaning to such a declaration of nonaggression. After the exchange, I was glad that we had Stilwell's leadership and experience; without it, I think some of our members might have been misled into doing something that they would have later regretted.

Once the North Koreans realized that we were not going to openly endorse their plan, the mood turned even worse. They had apparently intended to arrange a news conference to announce our acceptance of the nonaggression proposal, and this had to be canceled. At one time it was strongly suggested that, if we would endorse their plan, we would be rewarded with a meeting with the Great Leader himself. Stilwell was unmoved, and the arms-control talks ended with no progress.

U.S.–North Korean Relations

A second topic that we discussed was how to improve U.S.–North Korean relations. Again, General Stilwell began the discussions with the observation that the improvement of relations with the United States figured prominently on the North Korean agenda. An essential step in achieving that goal, said Stilwell, would be an accelerated search for and return of America's dead from the Korean War.

Recounting the history of the search for American war dead, Stilwell recalled that, in the year following the signing of the armistice agreement, substantial efforts were made by both sides to recover and return the remains of North Korean, Chinese, and United Nations Command servicemen. In 1954 more than 4,000 remains of United Nations personnel, including 1,868 Americans, were returned. The remains of approximately 8,100 Americans were still missing on North Korean soil. Since then North Korea has been asked repeatedly to account for 2,253 U.N. prisoners of war who were not repatriated immediately after the armistice and were believed to have died in captivity. No action had ever been taken by North Korea.

Stilwell said that the Americans now sought a commitment from the DPRK to undertake a serious effort to search for war dead at the prison-camp locations previously identified by the United States. Given such a commitment, and the development of a program for search and recovery, he was confident that the United States would be willing to provide financing and technical assistance. As this was a multinational matter, the overall venue should be international. Stilwell suggested that this could be arranged through the International Red Cross or perhaps the United Nations.

Responding for the North Korean side, Mr. Song Ho Gyong noted that the armistice agreement obliged North Korea to search for the MIAs only during the first year after the signing of the agreement. Because this was a humanitarian issue, North Korea was willing to solve the issue independent of the agreement and had raised it in its contacts with the United States and with Congress. Song said that the DPRK proposed to establish a joint U.S.–North Korean committee that would search for and repatriate MIAs; therefore, the involvement of the Red Cross or the United Nations was not necessary. Song complained, however, that Stilwell was presenting this issue as a precondition for improved relations with the United States. This, he said, complicated matters because North Korea wanted improved relations without preconditions. Because it recognized the MIAs as an obstacle, however, it was willing to resolve the issue.[5]

Moving on to other issues, Mr. Li Hyong Chul of the DPRK group said that the United States and North Korea needed to increase their contacts and dialogue in order to achieve an improvement in their relations. He accused U.S. policy of being outdated. Given cooperation between the United States and the Soviet Union, the establishment of diplomatic relations between the Soviet Union and South Korea, and the ties between the United States and China, an end to America's "cold war" treatment of North Korea was now appropriate.

Li declared there was no reason for the United States and North Korea to remain enemies and called on the United States to enter into direct negotiations with the DPRK without preconditions so the armistice agreement could be replaced by a peace treaty. Such a resolution would enable the United States to withdraw its troops from South Korea under a timetable to be negotiated in the future.

By this time it was apparent that the North Korean objective continued to be to separate the United States from the ROK by establishing these bilateral mechanisms such as joint committees, direct negotiations, and a separate peace treaty, among others. Since this was counter to existing U.S. government policy, we were in no position to accept any of these proposals. Thus, the issue of improved U.S.–North Korean relations also concluded without any agreements.

Nuclear Energy and Weapons

The final and most important topic was now at hand. I had had some prior contact with the issue of North Korea's nuclear program. In the summer of 1989, as rumors of North Korean nuclear work spread, I was among the members of the U.S. Embassy in Seoul who made a request to Washington for a briefing. Soon personnel arrived from CIA headquarters, including intelligence and technical experts in the nuclear field. The information they presented showed very strong evidence that North Korea was indeed developing a nuclear-weapons capability. After a question-and-answer session, the senior American present made a strong request that this information not be leaked from the room, but, of course, newspapers circulated reports of the briefing within a day or two.[6]

The embassy naturally wanted to pursue a diplomatic approach to the issue, working through the International Atomic Energy Agency (IAEA) in an effort to cause the DPRK to give up its plan. A direct approach was also considered, but it was decided against this course of action for political reasons. As it turned out, this decision merely postponed the meetings that began with the North Koreans in New York in 1992.[7]

But in 1989 no one wanted to consider military action, though most of us believed it was a viable option, at least from a military standpoint. North Korea's nuclear facilities were not yet fully developed or protected and were vulnerable to air or missile attack. Our analysis was that the DPRK would not voluntarily give up this program without getting something substantial in return, and the lengthy diplomatic process would probably not be successful until the North was very close to, or at the actual stage of, producing a nuclear weapon. (This has proven to be an accurate estimate.) I do not believe that a quick preemptive strike of the type that Israel made on Iraq's nuclear facilities a few years earlier was ever seriously considered, even though in 1989 there was a fairly high chance of success.

Dr. Van Cleave, an expert on nuclear weapons, opened the discussion on this issue. He began by emphasizing the importance that the United States, and indeed most of the rest of the world, placed on the issue of nuclear nonproliferation. The evidence was clear, he said, that North Korea was trying to avoid its obligations under the 1968 Nuclear Nonproliferation Treaty by developing a capability to manufacture nuclear weapons.

Van Cleave next invited the North Koreans to clarify their policy and their intentions. He noted the effort and resources that North Korea was pouring into the construction and improvement of its Yongbyon nuclear complex, which already had two or three reactors and a probable plutonium reprocessing plant. Displaying a satellite picture of the complex, Van Cleave said he could identify a reactor capable of producing plutonium, a probable plutonium separation plant, and a possible enrichment plant. As he pointed out each of these facilities on the satellite photo, the North Koreans appeared startled, surprised, and nervous.

There was no indication that the DPRK was using this complex for the production of electricity or energy; instead, it appeared to be a weapons facility, Van Cleave declared. He asked the purpose of separating the fuel from the plutonium and reprocessing it if the purpose was peaceful and not for weapons production, noting that the answers to his questions bore importantly on the improvement of U.S.–North Korean relations. He noted too that North Korea was suspected of having chemical-weapons production facilities as well. All in all, North Korea seemed disturbingly interested in weapons of mass destruction. It was also producing ballistic missiles that could deliver such weapons and was selling them to threatening, irresponsible states such as Syria and Libya.

At no point did the North Koreans attempt to answer any of these questions or to clarify either their nuclear policies or their intentions. They were clearly shocked by the satellite picture but recovered quickly, describing it as an American "doctored" photograph that merely attempted to force North Korea to sign the IAEA safeguards agreement. When they were informed that it was not an American but a French satellite photo, the North Koreans had no response.

One of their team argued that the concept of nuclear inspections was scientifically and technically unsound. It was unfair, he said, for the United States to insist that North Korea allow its facilities to be inspected. The United States opposed only the acquisition of nuclear weapons by other, nonnuclear states, while they were free to have tens of thousands of weapons themselves. In this way the United States opposed only horizontal but not vertical proliferation.

Van Cleave again cautioned the North Koreans that the United States, and much of the rest of the world, took the issue of nonproliferation of nuclear weapons very seriously indeed. No other issue was more important between North Korea and the United States and its allies. He denied that the United States opposed only horizontal and not vertical proliferation. As an example, the United States had been engaged for two decades in negotiations to stop the vertical proliferation of nuclear weapons, Van Cleave said, noting the strategic-arms treaty with the Soviet Union that would reduce strategic offensive weapons and the agreement on intermediate-range nuclear forces in Europe. In addition to these agreements, Van Cleave pointed out that, in the years since the NPT was signed, the United States had unilaterally removed some eight thousand nuclear weapons from its own arsenal and removed over two thousand such weapons from Western Europe, before any arms-control agreements on those forces were in existence.

North Korea, Van Cleave charged, apparently was trying to avoid its obligations under the NPT by artificially linking U.S. nuclear arms to the issue as a condition for fulfilling those obligations. The NPT had no bearing on U.S. nuclear weapons policies except for the obligation not to transfer nuclear weapons or technology to nonnuclear states. If, of course, North Korea were to insist on continuing what appeared to be a nuclear weapons program and refused safeguard inspections, or if it sold nuclear materials, then U.S. nuclear policy would have to take such behavior into account.

Van Cleave further stated that the North Korean responses to his remarks were wholly evasive and unsatisfactory. If the NPT is so unfair and unequal, why then did North Korea sign it in the first place? Clearly, he suggested, it did so for political purposes contrary to those of the treaty. It was attempting both to evade the NPT and to use it as a bargaining tool. In this case even inspection of DPRK facilities might not be helpful, for it would not tell the world what North Korea's true intentions were regarding nuclear weapons.

At this point it was becoming clear that the conference had been a failure. We had gone to Pyongyang with no great expectations of success but had hoped that we might have found some flexibility on at least one of the issues. This had not been the case, and we would be returning to Washington empty handed. Still, I felt that the direct contact with the North Koreans had been important in demonstrating a legitimate American intent to solve some of the serious problems that still existed on the Korean peninsula even long after the conclusion of the Korean War. It also gave me a feeling that, although we were unsuccessful at the time, there might be more success in future talks.

One reason for this cautious optimism was a feeling that most of the North Koreans we were in contact with genuinely desired better relations with the United States. With the Cold War at an end, with both the Soviet Union and China having established relations with the ROK, the DPRK would have been foolish not to explore contacts with Washington. Yet, hampered by their inexperience in dealing with Americans and their lack of contact with the outside world, North Korean leaders were terribly inexpert at how to accomplish this. My strong impression was that even the more senior North Korean officials were highly compartmentalized in their knowledge; they tended to be well informed only in their own small area of specialization. They also at times seemed to be victims of their own propaganda, misinformation, and ideology. Neither their political system nor their education allowed them to develop the type of flexibility or independent thinking essential to compromise, and without compromise, it was difficult to make any real progress on such issues of mutual importance.

If nothing else as the conference ended, we now knew that North Korean strategy had not changed. It was still oriented toward separating the United States and ROK and using the nuclear issue as their major bargaining chip. It has now been more than a decade since this trip and the conference, and I have seen only a few indications in North Korean behavior since that lead me to believe that there has been any change in either their strategy or their ultimate objective.

CHAPTER 14

Doing Business with North Korea

F ollowing retirement from the U.S. Army, I began a second career as a business consultant to several American companies engaged in business ventures in Asia. Almost all of these companies were engaged in the sale of nondefense items—computer software, restaurant franchises, marine engines, ship propellers, and such—so it was a whole new experience. This business often brought me back to South Korea and other Asian countries, and I was able to see my many Korean friends from time to time. Most of my work centered on helping American companies find the right partners or local agents, setting up marketing plans, assisting in contract negotiations, and culturally adjusting to the Asian way of doing business.

In early 1996 a New York–based company contacted me expressing an interest in obtaining magnesite from North Korea. Magnesite is a mineral used in a number of commercial applications, particularly in the steel industry. Much of the world's supply of magnesite is located in northeast China and North Korea, and the company believed that it would be advantageous to open up the market in the latter. I was asked if I could assist in this project by lending consulting expertise. After gathering more information, I determined that the project was feasible and agreed to assist.

At the time, all American trade with North Korea was restricted, so the first order of business was to obtain U.S. government approval to deal with the North Koreans. This involved permission from both the State Department and the Treasury Department, since any potential business dealing with North Korea would have political implications and involve transfer of funds, both requiring an exception to policy. On a one-time-exception basis, we were eventually able to receive both departments' approval to proceed.

The next step was to contact the right people in Pyongyang, and in this we were assisted by the North Korean U.N. office in New York. After numerous phone calls, faxes, and several meetings, it was agreed that the North Koreans would send a delegation to New York to negotiate what would hopefully be the first commercial agreement between an American company and North Korea since before the Korean War. Our side agreed—without any assistance from the U.S. government—to act as host and sponsor, including paying all transportation and travel costs for the North Koreans, who were, of course, strapped for hard currency.

The DPRK delegation arrived in New York about the middle of June and was met at JFK Airport, assisted through customs and immigration, and taken to a hotel to rest prior to beginning talks the next day. Our guests were dressed conservatively in somewhat dated suits and ties, presumably of North Korean manufacture. Some wore Kim Il Sung buttons.

The following morning we introduced ourselves, made the customary opening statements, and exchanged relevant information. Our side included the company president, the director for international business, our legal counsel, representatives from operations and marketing, and myself. The North Korean side's senior representative and spokesman was Oh Tae Bong, secretary general of the DPRK Committee for the Promotion of International Trade. Oh Hung Muk, vice president of the Korea Magnesia Export Corporation, was the number-two man, and he was assisted by an older gentleman who was introduced as an operations specialist. Two other North Koreans attended, but they were given only brief introductions and did not participate in the substance of any of the meetings. Eventually I deduced that one was probably gathering technical information and that the other was a security type whose function was to watch the rest of the delegation. All were very serious and largely humorless, although Oh Tae Bong did loosen up some later on when I was able to spend some time alone with him.

We had allowed four days for the meetings: two for the normal proceedings and negotiations, one for a field trip to visit a steel plant in Pennsylvania—which would demonstrate how the magnesite was to be used by the company—and another to wrap up final details and issue a joint statement and press release. As the initial meeting began, it became evident that things might not go according to plan.

I had written an opening statement for the company president to deliver that included some language that would translate well into Korean and was designed to get things off to a good start. It seemed to work; the other side nodded appreciably at the right times during the translation of the comments and made all the right gestures. It was now time for Oh Tae Bong to respond. Putting his prepared remarks aside for the moment, he looked at his host directly and told him how much he appreciated his opening words, which he said were much kinder and gracious than he had expected. Oh said he looked forward to a unique opportunity to negotiate a historical agreement in an atmosphere in which both sides were treated with respect and equality, and he made some other pleasant remarks. Then he picked up his papers and said it was time to read his official opening statement. From the text of the official statement, it was difficult to believe that this was the same individual who had seconds earlier been so gracious. The official statement sounded more like a propaganda harangue at Panmunjom. At least thirty minutes were devoted to the glories of the Great Leader (the now-deceased Kim Il Sung) and "Dear Leader" (Kim Il Sung's designated successor, Kim Jong Il). There were several nasty references to American imperialists, war-mongering American hegemonists, and the like. After two glasses of water and about forty minutes, Oh finished his diatribe, then looked across the table and said matter of factly, "Okay, now lets talk about magnesite."

The negotiations from this point took on an us-versus-them tone. By the end of the day, it was clear that the North Koreans had little authority even to negotiate a simple business contract. They were required to telephone Pyongyang each evening for instructions, then we would debate various elements of our conflicting positions. Information that was open in our society was a state secret in theirs, so we were unable to obtain even rudimentary knowledge of their production capacity, port facilities, technical specifications of the product, or any other data that we needed to make an informed business decision. Further, it rapidly became apparent that Oh Tae Bong (who we referred to as "Big Oh") and Oh Hung Muk (who we referred to as "Little Oh") were personally hostile to each other and on opposite sides of almost every issue. They actually spent more time arguing with each other than with us. "Big Oh" had the mission of negotiating a successful contract that would make him and his government look good. As the production manager, though, "Little Oh" would be the one who actually had to mine the product, find a way to transport and deliver it to port, meet deadlines, and fulfill all other contractual obligations in a country that had a deteriorating infrastructure, massive fuel shortages, and other impediments. Any previous vision we might have had of monolithic socialists speaking with one mind soon disappeared.

There were some problems as well beyond the conference proceedings. The North Koreans were suspicious to a point verging on paranoia. They would not answer even basic personal questions such as where they had been born and raised, where they had gone to school, and whether they were married and had children. More seriously, they were convinced that their rooms were bugged and insisted on changing hotels. The initial host hotel raised no objection, perhaps in part because the North Koreans engaged in the practice (common in their native *yogwans*) of walking in the halls between their rooms in their pajamas or underwear, which was undoubtedly disconcerting to some of the well-heeled American guests. Yet hotel space in New York City in the summer is sometimes hard to find, and it proved no small task to secure rooms at an alternate establishment. When we paid the bill at the first hotel, it not only included a hefty minibar bill but also charges for twenty-five "adult" movies. We now understood why our guests had so frequently tended to nod off during the meetings, which we had initially assumed was due to jet lag.

Despite these distractions, by the end of the second day, we had outlined the basics of an agreement, which included an understanding of product quality, acceptable quality-control measures, price, and delivery terms and conditions. Based on this tentative agreement, which still needed to be approved in Pyongyang, the scheduled field trip went forward on day three. The only mishap occurred when "Big Oh," who had received several deliveries of gifts and flowers from a surprising number of admirers in the New York area, received a particularly impressive floral display, which was somehow placed in the sedan in which he was traveling during the field trip. "Little Oh," who was sharing the car, promptly inspected the card, saw that it was addressed to "Big Oh," and tossed what must have been a three-hundred-dollar floral display out of the window and onto the streets of New York.

By the final day we had prepared a draft of the joint statement, a press release, and a contract based on what we had agreed to earlier. The North Koreans, especially "Big Oh," were initially preoccupied with the wording of the joint statement, and the entire morning was spent satisfying their concerns. The afternoon was to be the contract signing, and the company chairman had arrived to participate in this momentous occasion. Following lunch, we prepared for the ceremony, complete with champagne and appropriate toasts. "Big Oh" then announced that there were some "problems" with the contract and turned to "Little Oh" to handle the details. "Little Oh," who had never wanted an agreement to begin with, then began to object to every detail in it, including those items on which we had been in agreement from the start. He insisted on a higher price, objected to quality-control testing as an infringement on "national pride," and refused to agree to the delivery timetable we had earlier established. He also insisted on being paid at least half the contract value in advance, with that amount to be deposited in a private account in China. We were clearly back to square one, and the ceremony was abruptly cancelled.

That evening it appeared that there would be no contract, but we had previously scheduled a final dinner at a very nice Chinese restaurant and decided to go ahead with those plans. The company chairman was the host, and the DPRK ambassador to the United Nations was in attendance as well. The mood was subdued, with "Big Oh" and "Little Oh" seated as far from each other as possible. Throughout the meal, they periodically glared at each other. Once during a toast and remarks by "Big Oh," "Little Oh" pretended to doze off, even producing a few snoring sounds for the purpose of showing further disrespect. At the end of the evening, the North Korean U.N. ambassador pulled both "Ohs" to the corner and spoke to them firmly and authoritatively in Korean. As we prepared to break up, "Big Oh" suddenly announced that his side wanted to meet again. At about 10:00 P.M. on the final night, we returned to company headquarters to reopen the negotiations.

Even with this added emphasis, "Little Oh" continued to do everything possible to delay and disrupt the proceedings. Well after midnight, I finally pulled him aside during a break to explain, in Korean, that if we could not sign a contract in the next hour, it would be impossible for us to get their group to the airport early enough to have time to shop at the duty-free store, where we had intended on buying departure gifts of premium Scotch and cigarettes. Whether it was this final enticement or the thought of spending the next winter on a work farm somewhere in the North Korean boondocks is unclear, but "Little Oh" soon dropped his objections, signed the contract, and we went back to the hotel for a couple of hours of rest before leaving for JFK.

In retrospect, the magnesite-contract adventure was what might be called a character-building experience. The North Koreans were eventually only able to fulfill part of their contractual responsibilities, but it was a useful meeting in that we learned more about their motivations and what can realistically be expected when doing business with the DPRK. In the period since that event, I have had some other dealings with the North Koreans, which went more smoothly, probably because of lowered expectations. I have also formed some opinions about the best way of dealing with them in the future.

CHAPTER 15

Final Reflections

I t has now been almost forty years since I first became acquainted with Korea. Most of the people described in the preceding chapters have gone on to other pursuits and activities. Some are still involved with Korea or Asia in general; others are retired. Of the ambassadors and senior military officers with whom I served, all were faced with different problems and events. Each reacted with professionalism, and each performed a valuable service to his country. Americans and Koreans alike owe them a debt of gratitude.

In the decade of the 1970s, Ambassadors Philip Habib and Richard Sneider, both of whom are now deceased, were instrumental in thwarting a South Korean program to develop nuclear weapons. Gen. Richard Stilwell, a mentor and friend who provided critical leadership during Operation Paul Bunyan, was instrumental in policy formulation in Asia for several years after his retirement. He died a few months after our return from the North Korea trip. Ambassador William Gleysteen faced perhaps the toughest issues of any ambassador under whom I served; after leaving government service, he went on to become president of the Japan Society in New York for several years. I saw him two years ago at an academic conference, and we relived the old days of a presidential assassination, a military coup and various intrigue, and the Kwangju massacre. Gen. John Wickham went on to eventually become chief of staff of the U.S. Army; he is now retired in Arizona. Bob Brewster, the U.S. Embassy's senior intelligence official and my collaborator during the events of 1979–80, died of cancer in 1983.

In the 1980s Ambassador Richard "Dixie" Walker served with distinction for almost six years during a turbulent period; his quiet diplomacy and pleasing personality were important factors in reestablishing harmonious relations between the government of Chun Doo Hwan and the Reagan administration following the stormy period of the Carter years. He remains active in Korean affairs as ambassador-in-residence at the University of South Carolina's Walker Institute of International Studies, and I still see him often. Ambassador James Lilley's strong leadership in 1987–88 headed off several potential crises, and his tenure coincided with the first peaceful transfer of power and democratic presidential election in Korean history. He is presently a senior fellow with the American Enterprise Institute in Washington and a frequent contributor on Asian matters on network television and in major news magazines. Ambassador Donald Gregg was a driving force for reducing anti-Americanism in South Korea and instrumental in refocusing and expanding the U.S.-Korean relationship. Since his retirement from government service, he has been the chairman of the Korea Society, headquartered in New York, and has built that organization from infancy to major-league status.

On the Korean side, fate has played a rather remarkable hand. Chun Doo Hwan, the leader of the 12/12 coup, became president of South Korea in September, 1980. His tenure as president was reasonably successful in most respects. He appointed capable and experienced people to the government and was a competent executive. The economy flourished during his administration, and many Koreans paid him grudging respect, despite the fact that his regime was highly authoritarian in nature. During the presidency of Kim Young Sam, he was arrested and charged with multiple crimes, including mutiny, treason, and corruption in connection with the 12/12 incident and the Kwangju massacre. Sentenced to death and to pay a huge fine, he was eventually pardoned in December, 1997.

Roh Tae Woo, Chun's classmate and lifelong friend, succeeded him as president. Roh was the first Korean president in over a generation to be selected in an open and honest election. His tenure included the successful hosting of the Seoul Olympics in 1988 but was marked by serious corruption. He was arrested at the same time as Chun and found guilty of similar crimes, receiving a sentence of more than twenty years in prison and a fine of over 150 million dollars. He also was pardoned in 1997.

Kim Young Sam succeeded Roh as president. One of his first acts in office was to purge the military, ensuring that the armed services would never be able to mount another coup. His administration was plagued by corruption and without notable accomplishments.

Kim Dae Jung survived six years' imprisonment, several assassination attempts, numerous restrictions on his political activity, and foreign exile. In 1997 he was elected to the presidency. One of his first official acts was to pardon former Presidents Chun and Rho as well as their supporters, the very group that had sentenced him to death in 1980. Despite the fact that he was not held in especially high esteem by some senior American officials during the 1970s and 1980s, U.S.-Korean relations during his administration have been generally harmonious. Kim Dae Jung has received high marks by most international observers, and in 2000 he was awarded the Nobel Peace Prize.

Lessons Learned

My experience over the years has resulted in several "lessons learned." One of these is the importance of training legitimate area experts. This is relatively easy when dealing with European countries, where the languages and culture are not that different from our own. In Asia, however, the development of true area experts who are knowledgeable of the history, politics, economic patterns, culture, and language of a specific country is a lengthy and expensive undertaking. When I reached the rank of colonel, there were perhaps two or three other officers of that rank in the army who were legitimate Korea experts. Today, with a smaller service, there are probably only one or two. Neither the navy nor the air force has any programs to develop area specialists. Nor is the situation much better in the State Department, which has only one or two senior career diplomats capable of conducting an intelligent conversation in Korean. Americans are notorious for being poor linguists and insensitive to the cultures of other countries, but surely we can invest the time and effort necessary to develop experienced and competent specialists.

Regarding the conduct of our foreign policy, I have learned several general principles. First, we need to be aware of our limitations when imposing traditional American values and institutions on other countries. This is particularly true in Asia, where Confucian values and different political and economic factors exist. In most Asian countries, particularly the Koreas, internal factors are far more important in determining behavior or the manner in which a particular decision may be made. By understanding those influences better, diplomats and senior military officers will be more successful in working with their counterparts toward mutually successful outcomes. In the process, they also will be more successful in furthering U.S. goals and interests.

Second, diplomacy is more successful when conducted in a low-key and nonconfrontational manner. The many efforts during the Carter years to effect South Korean behavior were unsuccessful in part because we were too direct and forceful, particularly in the human rights area. Carter's uncoordinated and poorly timed troop-withdrawal policy was ultimately a failure, sabotaged in some cases by his own subordinates. The Reagan years, which focused on low-key, private representations, were ultimately successful. The

Reagan team was able to witness the first democratically elected government since 1960 due not only to a changed internal political environment but also helped by the private representations of effective ambassadors such as "Dixie" Walker and Jim Lilley.

Third, I have been impressed by the importance of personal relations and personalities and the role these factors play in successful diplomacy. This is particularly true in Asia, where an in-depth understanding of the relationships between individuals and their sometimes-hidden agendas is often difficult to acquire. In retrospect, some have speculated that the outcome of the 12/12 incident and subsequent events might have been different if the blunt and forceful Chun Doo Hwan had been dealing with an equally blunt and forceful Ambassador Lilley and the highly respected Gen. John Vessey rather than the capable but somewhat mild-mannered and cerebral Gleysteen and Wickham, Vessey's successor. I am not certain that it would have produced a different outcome, but that the question is even raised is testimony to the importance of personalities in diplomacy.

Fourth, we need to learn and profit from our mistakes. Although the ultimate result might have been the same, I believe we made several errors in dealing with the events of 1979–80. In retrospect, we should have paid more attention to intelligence reporting in the days between the assassination of Park Chung Hee and the 12/12 coup. Specifically, the pending reassignment of Chun Doo Hwan to an unattractive position far removed from his power base in Seoul should have been a tip-off of problems to come. We should have opened a channel to the military moderates immediately after the assassination but never did. Instead, our focus remained too concentrated on the North Korean threat. Over the entire period from October, 1979, until Chun became president in September, 1980, there was never any hard evidence that the North intended to take military advantage of a confusing situation in the South. I also believe that it was a mistake to postpone the security consultative meeting in response to Chun's power grab. Not only is it generally questionable policy to link security issues to political events, but this move also alienated many of the moderates in the ROK Army, unnecessarily antagonized those in the civilian government whose influence we needed, and lessened the ability of the Department of Defense to favorably influence the situation.

Lastly, we should have been more aggressive in ensuring that the American position and views regarding 12/12, Kwangju, and the power grab by Chun Doo Hwan were available to the Korean public. We failed to use all the information-dissemination tools at our disposal, and to this day many

Koreans hold the United States at least partially reasonable for those unpleasant events in modern Korean history.

Thoughts on North Korea

In the years following my retirement from the army, I have also formed some opinions concerning the North Koreans based on my dealing with them both in a semiofficial context during the conference in Pyongyang and in subsequent dealings over the past few years.

First, they are more fragmented internally than is commonly thought. This began following the death of Kim Il Sung and is manifested in conflicting attitudes among some of their leadership, examples including the military versus certain "moderates" in the foreign ministry, and the commercial policymakers in Pyongyang versus production managers in the field, who are charged with carrying out policy decisions with virtually no resources allocated for the task. The breach between Pyongyang and the countryside has grown with the prolonged economic and food crises, and at some point the authority of the central government may be eroded.

Second, they are very compartmentalized, even at the higher levels of government. Thus, a senior officer charged with North Korean political policy may be quite expert in that field but have virtually no expertise in commercial, economic, or military matters that heavily affect his primary area of responsibility. Contrast this with a modern American military officer or foreign service officer, whose depth of knowledge and appreciation of a multidisciplined approach to problem solving is far broader. If our own officials are sometimes criticized for being "a mile wide and an inch deep," I would submit that my experience with the North Koreans tends to expose them as "an inch wide and an inch deep."

Third, at least some North Koreans are genuinely sincere in their desire for a better relationship with the United States. They are cognizant of the benefits that a better political relationship and access to technology and commercial contacts will ultimately bring to their country. Regrettably they have painted themselves into a corner internally, from which there is probably no escape. A true liberalization of the economy and the social system to the extent that it would allow access to the benefits of a market economy and the western technological revolution is virtually impossible. To do so would be for the North Korean leadership to admit to their population that, for the past five and a half decades, the people have been victims of the "big lie."

I am uncertain what this means in terms of our ultimate relations with the North. Until recently, those relations were better today than they were when I last traveled to Pyongyang. We continue to have several bilateral and multilateral forums in which we are involved with the North Koreans, and South Korean president Kim Dae Jung's "Sunshine Policy" has been endorsed by his successor, although its survival is very much in doubt given North Korea's apparent determination to pursue an active nuclear weapons development program. Nonetheless, my experience tends to make me a cautious believer in a policy of constructive engagement, with limitations. For example, it is difficult to justify continuing aid to the DPRK in light of their missile sales to the Middle East, their consistently antagonistic behavior, and their dangerous brinksmanship with the nuclear issue; at some point there needs to be a quid pro quo.

The leading role in dealing with North Korea may by necessity come from the United States, but it should be closely coordinated with South Korea and our other allies in that region. It is the ROK that will eventually accept the burden of political reconciliation, helping the North out of its economic miseries, rebuilding its deteriorating infrastructure, and perhaps most importantly, reeducating its population. This does not mean that the United States should abrogate our right to deal directly with the North on any issue we see fit, nor does it preclude bilateral initiatives. We should also insist that the United States be consulted closely on any major new ROK-DPRK policy initiatives, for we have important strategic interests in the area as well as almost forty thousand troops deployed on the Korean peninsula. Any final settlement of the deep issues that separate the two Koreas, however, will as a matter of practical necessity ultimately have the full support of the Koreans themselves, both North and South.

I have been fortunate to enjoy a career and opportunities that few army officers have been able to experience. It has involved contact and friendships with interesting people from all walks of life and a firsthand view of many of the events that have shaped modern Korean history. South Korea is now a different place from the country I experienced during the 1960s, 1970s, and 1980s. Its economy has recovered from the downturn of the late 1990s, and the ROK is now a prospering and confident democracy. Most of the credit for this metamorphosis should rightly go to hardworking and determined Koreans. We Americans have also played a role, however, and have remained steadfast friends and allies during some difficult times. Perhaps that is our best achievement in the past, and hopefully it will be a future one as well.

NOTES

Abbreviations

BM   Brzezinski Materials, Jimmy Carter Presidential Library, Atlanta, Ga.
DHM   Donated Historical Materials, Zbigniew Brzezinski Collection, Jimmy Carter
      Presidential Library, Atlanta, Ga.
GRFL Gerald R. Ford Presidential Library, Ann Arbor, Mich.
NYT   *New York Times*
WP   *Washington Post*

Author's Preface

1. William H. Gleysteen Jr., *Massive Entanglement, Marginal Influence: Carter and Korea in Crisis* (Washington, D.C.: Brookings Institution Press, 1999); John A. Wickham, *Korea on the Brink: From the '12/12 Incident' to the Kwangju Uprising, 1979–1980* (Washington, D.C: National Defense University Press, 1999).

Chapter 1. Preparation

1. These developments are well covered in Don Oberdorfer, *The Two Koreas: A Contemporary History* (Reading, Mass.: Addison-Wesley, 1997), pp. 11–46.

Chapter 2. Into the Fray

1. For a useful secondary account, see Oberdorfer, *Two Koreas*, pp. 68–74. For discussions of the issues relating to nuclear weapons on the Korean peninsula in the 1970s, see Joo-Hong Nam, *America's Commitment to South Korea: The First Decade of the Nixon Doctrine* (New York: Cambridge University Press, 1986), pp. 73–108; and Peter Hayes, *Pacific Powderkeg: American Nuclear Dilemmas in Korea* (Lexington, Mass.: D. C. Heath, 1991), pp. 53–86, 199–207.
2. For substantial documentation on the nuclear issue, see Boxes A1, A3, Temporary Parallel Files, Office of the Assistant to the President for National Security Affairs, 1974–77, GRFL.
3. See *WP*, June 10, 1975, p. A8.
4. For a good secondary account focusing on high-level Washington decision making, see Oberdorfer, *Two Koreas*, pp. 74–83.
5. Substantial documentation on Washington's deliberations on this issue is available in Box 1, National Security Adviser, Presidential Country Files for East Asia and the Pacific, 1974–1977, Country File Korea (15), GRFL.
6. This story was widely circulated following Operation Paul Bunyan and is recounted in John K. Singlaub, *Hazardous Duty: An American Soldier in the Twentieth Century* (New York: Summit, 1991), p. 376.

7. Regardless of the true location of the helicopter, the conventional wisdom in Washington was that it had no business being in the JSA, especially since troops had been withdrawn and the mission accomplished. This incident is mentioned briefly in ibid., p. 378.

Chapter 3. Rise of the Troop-Withdrawal Issue

1. For an excellent survey of Carter's efforts to redirect U.S. foreign policy, see Gaddis Smith, *Morality, Reason, and Power: American Diplomacy in the Carter Years* (New York: Hill and Wang, 1986).
2. President Ford's election committee kept a record of Carter's statements along these lines. They can be found in Research Office, Carter Quotes File, Box H28, President Ford Committee Records, 1975–76, GRFL.

    Carter's ideas were not totally out of step with the thinking of some leading U.S. officials going back as far as the Eisenhower administration. In a National Security Council meeting on April 21, 1955, for example, President Eisenhower, who also doubted the feasibility of maintaining substantial numbers of U.S. troops in Europe over the long term, showed sympathy toward keeping merely "token forces" in Korea. U.S. Department of State, *Foreign Relations of the United States, 1955–1957*, vol. 23, pt. 2 (Washington, D.C.: Government Printing Office, 1993), p. 71. Fourteen years later Pres. Richard Nixon expressed to his national security advisor an interest in reducing U.S. forces in Korea to a sufficient "air and sea presence . . . necessary for the kind of retaliatory strike which we have planned" if North Korea attacked the South. Nixon to Henry Kissinger, Nov. 24, 1969, Box 341, Subject Files, National Security Council Files, Nixon Presidential Materials Project, U.S. National Archives II, College Park, Md.
3. This story is told from the perspective of USFK in Singlaub, *Hazardous Duty*, pp. 385–405. For a well-informed secondary account, see Oberdorfer, *Two Koreas*, pp. 84–105. For a briefer account sympathetic to Carter, see Selig Harrison, *Korean Endgame: A Strategy for Reunification and U.S. Disengagement* (Princeton, N.J.: Princeton University Press, 2002), pp. 178–79.
4. In a proposed text for a joint communiqué at the end of the Ford-Park meeting, the South Koreans included the following statement: "The two presidents noted that the increasing military capabilities of North Korea continue to pose a serious threat to the security of the Republic of Korea." See Seoul Embassy to the Secretary of State, Nov. 11, 1974, Box 7, Press Secretary's Files, GRFL. This statement was not in the actual joint communiqué issued on November 22, 1975. See *Department of State Bulletin* 71 (Dec. 23, 1974): 877–78. The author does not believe there was a direct connection between the Ford-Park meeting and the subsequent U.S. Army study.
5. Back in Seoul, Vessey told others the same thing. See Singlaub, *Hazardous Duty*, p. 383.
6. Ibid., p. 384.
7. On May 11 he wired the JCS that the "option calling for total withdrawal of ground forces by Dec 80 carries significant risk to peace on [the] Korean peninsula. . . . ROK forces would not be able to achieve and maintain offsetting capabilities in this time frame." Of the options with which he was presented, the one projecting complete withdrawal by July, 1982, would "minimize risks," but even this one would "require maximum flexibility and latitude [for the field commander] to adjust [the] withdrawal schedule to assure ability to accomplish missions and maintain ROK confidence to defend themselves." Six days later he told the JCS that "withdrawal

of U.S. ground forces from Korea will have a profound effect upon both allies and adversaries throughout the Pacific. This pullback will be perceived as evidence of slackening U.S. resolve to play a decisive role in Asia. No combination of actions will offset the psychological, political, economic, and military impact of our withdrawal." CINCPAC to JCS, May 11, 17, 1977, Box 44, Country File, National Security Affairs, BM.

8. For Singlaub's account, see *Hazardous Duty*, pp. 385–89. For Saar's article, see *WP*, May 19, 1977, p. A1.

9. Singlaub, *Hazardous Duty*, pp. 389–98.

10. For the record of the open portion of the hearings, see U.S. Congress, House of Representatives, Committee on Armed Services, *Hearings on Review of the Policy Decision to Withdraw United States Ground Forces from Korea before the Investigations Subcommittee*, 95th Cong., 1st, 2d sess., May 25, 1977 (Washington, D.C.: Government Printing Office, 1978).

11. The *New York Times*, which had previously supported Carter's plan for withdrawal and his disciplining of Singlaub, gave wide coverage of the issue as it emerged in Congress. See *NYT*, May 29, 1977, sec. 4, pp. 1, 3; May 30, 1977, p. 2; June 6, 1977, pp. 1, 5; June 8, 1977, p. 20; May 17, 1977, p. 3; May 18, 1977, p. 18; May 19, 1977, sec. 4, p. 17. In July the paper did a public-opinion survey with CBS News and found that 58 percent of those interviewed were in favor of retaining some U.S. troops in the ROK on an indefinite basis. *NYT*, July 29, 1977, p. 22. Stilwell's views received major attention in *Newsweek*, June 6, 1977, p. 51.

12. Brown and Habib to the President, May 28, 1977, Box 43, Country File, National Security Affairs, BM. For a mixed but basically pessimistic assessment of the situation in Congress after Habib testified before the Senate Foreign Relations Committee on June 10, see Zbigniew Brzezinski [national security adviser] to the President, June 10, 1977, ibid. By the end of the month, Mike Armacost, an aide to Brzezinski on the National Security Council, was privately expressing outrage that the Defense Department had released to the House Armed Services Committee a series of top-secret messages from General Vessey to the JCS challenging the withdrawal policy. See Armacost to Brzezinski, June 29, 1977, ibid. On July 21 Brzezinski reported to the president that "the reaction of Congressional leaders to Harold Brown's Korean briefing this morning was very chilly. . . . Sentiment in favor of troop withdrawal is at best lukewarm and passive. This is bad enough, but worse yet are the indications that it will be very difficult to secure the needed military assistance to upgrade ROK defenses as we withdraw." See ibid.

13. Part of this story is told in Singlaub, *Hazardous Duty*, p. 425. It was also related to the author by one of General Vessey's senior staff officers shortly after he returned from Washington.

14. For more on Holbrooke and the withdrawal issue, see Gleysteen, *Massive Entanglement*, pp. 18–19. Although later the U.S. ambassador to South Korea, Gleysteen was initially Holbrooke's deputy in the State Department. For evidence of dissent within the administration, see the minutes of the Policy Review Committee meeting, Apr. 21, 1977, Box 24, Subject File, DHM. Holbrooke, Abramowitz, and Armacost were all in attendance at this meeting.

15. The author was not personally involved with the activities of Holbrooke. This account is developed from several other published versions. For more information and background, see Gleysteen, *Massive Entanglement*, pp. 20–30; Oberdorfer, *Two Koreas*, pp. 89–94; and Hayes, *Pacific Powderkeg*, pp. 75–84.

16. Habib had been seeking a review of U.S. force levels in Korea since at least 1974,

when he was the American ambassador in Seoul. See "Secretary's Staff Meeting, January 25, 1974," Jan. 28, 1974, Transcripts of Secretary of State Henry A. Kissinger's Staff Meetings, National Security Archives, Washington, D.C. Back in Washington in 1976 as assistant secretary of state for East Asian and Pacific Affairs, Habib pushed for U.S. troop withdrawals. See "Secretary's Staff Meeting, June 1, 1976," ibid.

17. For an expression of concern on this issue by one who formally supported Carter's policy, see Brzezinski to the President, Apr. 18, 1978, Box 36, Subject File, DHM.

18. Unlike PRM-13, PRM-45 was widely staffed within the State Department, Department of Defense, the intelligence community, and the National Security Council, in many cases down to the working level. Its existence was well known within the Washington bureaucracy and Seoul embassy staff, and it was a much more professional product than PRM-13.

Chapter 4. To Korea Again

1. For the background, see Gleysteen, *Massive Entanglement*, pp. 35–45; and various materials, Boxes 43, 44, Country File, National Security Affairs, BM. By April, 1979, Brzezinski was advising Carter to ease away from his stance on troop withdrawal. See Brzezinski to the President [National Security Council Weekly Report 94], Apr. 12, 1979, Box 42, Subject File, DHM.

2. See Gleysteen, *Massive Entanglement*, p. 46. Carter took extensive notes on his meeting with Park Chung Hee. Nicholas Platt, a National Security Council staffer, did as well, and his account was developed into a "Memorandum of Conversation" dated July 5. Both men's writings are found in Box 2, President's Personal Foreign Affairs File, Plains File, Jimmy Carter Presidential Library, Atlanta, Ga.

3. Several varying accounts of this event circulated after the summit. For Gleysteen's, see *Massive Entanglement*, pp. 47–48. See also Hayes, *Pacific Powderkeg*, p. 82.

4. On July 12 Brzezinski wrote to Carter that "the time has come for a decision on U.S. ground force withdrawals from the ROK." He proceeded to weigh the options and suggest that the president either (1) put all further consideration of withdrawals in abeyance until 1981 or (2) withdraw 4,300 men by the end of 1980, with consideration of further withdrawals held off until 1981. Carter chose the former option, which was announced on July 20. See Box 20, Subject File, DHM. See also Gleysteen, *Massive Entanglement*, pp. 49–50.

5. For elaboration on the matter by the ambassador, see Gleysteen, *Massive Entanglement*, pp. 51–52.

Chapter 5. The Park Assassination and Its Aftermath

1. U.S. Embassy, Seoul, U.S. Information Service Press Office, "U.S. Government Statement on the Events in Kwangju, Republic of Korea, in May 1980," June 19, 1989, p. 5. This document is published in full in Wickham, *Korea on the Brink*, pp. 193–212.

2. For Ambassador Gleysteen's treatment of this issue, see *Massive Entanglement*, pp. 57–62, 207–10.

3. Wickham, *Korea on the Brink*, p. 197.

4. For Ambassador Gleysteen's account, see *Massive Entanglement*, p. 67. For the text of the "scope paper" prepared for Vance on his Korea visit, see Secretary of State to American Embassy, Seoul, Nov. 1, 1979, "State Department Documents Declassified on June 19, 1993," copy in editor's possession.

5. For a description of Chung by Gen. John A. Wickham, the commander of U.S. Forces Korea at the time, see Wickham, *Korea on the Brink*, p. 12.
6. Detailed discussions of these events are found in chapters 6 and 9.
7. For General Wickham's account on this matter, see *Korea on the Brink*, pp. 38, 49–51. Ambassador Gleysteen does not make it clear whether or not he was aware of the rumors prior to 12/12. See Gleysteen, *Massive Entanglement*, p. 79.
8. Wickham, *Korea on the Brink*, p. 197.
9. Ibid., p. 51.

Chapter 6. The 12/12 Incident

1. General Choi was a Class 11 KMA classmate and confidant of Chun Doo Hwan. He was not involved directly in the 12/12 events but substantially profited from them. Within two days he was promoted from deputy intelligence chief of the army (assistant to G-2) to the J-2 position, the senior military intelligence officer in Korea.
2. For Wickham's account of events in the Bunker, see *Korea on the Brink*, pp. 53–66; for Gleysteen's perspective, see *Massive Entanglement*, pp. 78–82.
3. Wickham, *Korea on the Brink*, p. 198.

Chapter 7. Aftermath of 12/12

1. Itaewon, a section of Seoul located adjacent to the Yongsan army base, remains a popular entertainment and shopping area for foreigners.
2. Gleysteen, *Massive Entanglement*, pp. 82–84.
3. Gleysteen says that the meeting was "at my request." Ibid., p. 84.
4. The ambassador was held in high regard in Washington. Early in the year, National Security Council staffer Nicholas Platt wrote to Brzezinski that, "since assuming his post in Seoul this summer [Gleysteen] has taken hold as one of our strongest Ambassadors in Asia." In particular Platt commended Gleysteen on his handling of visiting members of Congress. See Platt to Brzezinski, Jan. 24, 1979, Box 44, Country File, National Security Affairs, BM. Finessing American legislators, of course, was an entirely different matter than confronting an aspiring military dictator on his own turf.
5. Gleysteen, *Massive Entanglement*, pp. 84–85. For a highly sanitized account of the meeting, see Gleysteen to the Secretary of State, Dec. 15, 1980, Box 44, Country File, National Security Affairs, BM.
6. See Mark L. Clifford, *Troubled Tiger: Businessmen, Bureaucrats, and Generals in South Korea* (Armonk, N.Y.: M. E. Sharpe, 1994), chaps. 9, 13.
7. Wickham, *Korea on the Brink*, p. 199.
8. On the 1987 case, see William Stueck, "Democratization in Korea: The United States Role, 1980 and 1987," *International Journal of Korean Studies* 2, no. 1 (fall/winter, 1998): 14–15.
9. Wickham was approached by a more senior officer. See Wickham, *Korea on the Brink*, pp. 77–79. Apparently Gleysteen was not approached directly, but he was informed of the plot(s). See Gleysteen, *Massive Entanglement*, pp. 93–96.

Chapter 8. Prelude to Kwangju

1. See *NYT*, Feb. 29, 1980, p. 3; Mar. 1, 1980, p. 3; Mar. 8, 1980, p. 20.
2. Gleysteen, *Massive Entanglement*, pp. 99–105. Gleysteen's account is consistent with

his reporting at the time as reflected in "State Department Documents Declassified on June 19, 1993," copies in editor's possession.

3. For Wickham's account of this meeting, see *Korea on the Brink*, pp. 114–18.
4. Wickham implies that the meeting came about as a result of hints from an intermediary, Gen. Mun Hyong Tae, now retired from the army and a member of the National Assembly Defense Committee. See Wickham, *Korea on the Brink*, pp. 111, 114–18.
5. Gleysteen, *Massive Entanglement*, pp. 106–109.
6. See ibid., pp. 109–11.
7. Gleysteen does not acknowledge the dissent of the U.S. military. See ibid.
8. Ibid., pp. 111–12.
9. See ibid., pp. 115–17; and Gleysteen to the Secretary of State, May 9, 1980, in "State Department Documents Declassified on June 19, 1993," copy in editor's possession.
10. Wickham, *Korea on the Brink*, pp. 200–201.
11. *InSam Cha* is a unique Korean tea derived from ginseng roots.
12. Wickham, *Korea on the Brink*, pp. 121–24, 201.
13. Ibid., p. 201.
14. Ibid.; Gleysteen, *Massive Entanglement*, p. 118.

Chapter 9. Kwangju and Its Aftermath

1. Wickham, *Korea on the Brink*, p. 202.
2. For a brief account of events covered in this chapter, see Oberdorfer, *Two Koreas*, pp. 124–30; and Nam Koon Woo, *South Korean Politics: The Search for Political Consensus and Stability* (New York: University Press of America, 1989), pp. 221–24. For a sharp critique of U.S. policy, see Tim Shorrock, "U.S. Knew of South Korean Crackdown: Ex-Leaders Go on Trial in Seoul," *Journal of Commerce*, Feb. 27, 1996, p. 1; and Tim Shorrock, "The U.S. Role in Korea in 1979 and 1980," *Korea Web Weekly*, Oct. 1997 <http://www.kimsoft.com/korea//kwangju3.htm>. For a more moderate critique, see James Fowler, "The United States and South Korean Democratization," *Political Science Quarterly* 114, no. 2 (Oct., 1999): 265–88. For a less critical analysis, see Stueck, "Democratization in Korea," pp. 1–26.
3. Gleysteen, *Massive Entanglement*, pp. 121–22.
4. Ibid., 121–22; Wickham, *Korea on the Brink*, 203; Gleysteen to Secretary of State, May 17, 1980, Box 44, Country File, National Security Affairs, BM.
5. Gleysteen, *Massive Entanglement*, p. 122.
6. Ibid., pp. 123–24.
7. Some accounts of this period tend to paint Brewster as a supporter of Chun. In the author's experience this was not the case. Brewster was always evenhanded in his approach. For a contrary view, see Wickham, *Korea on the Brink*, pp. 33, 39, 56, 79.
8. Ibid., p. 203.
9. Ibid., p. 205. For various eyewitness accounts of events in Kwangju, see Henry Scott-Stokes and Lee Jai Eui, eds., *The Kwangju Uprising: Eyewitness Press Accounts of Korea's Tiananmen* (Armonk, N.Y.: M. E. Sharpe, 2000).
10. Wickham, *Korea on the Brink*, p. 205.
11. See Gleysteen, Report to the Secretary of State, May 21, 1980, Box 44, Country File, National Security Affairs, BM.
12. Ambassador Gleysteen makes the following statement on this general issue: "We had a strong, Korean-speaking officer in the Political Section, Spence Richardson, who visited Kwangju after the crisis and prepared a solid report. I now fault myself

for not sending him or someone else to Kwangju as soon as I learned about the severity of the crisis." See Gleysteen, *Massive Entanglement*, pp. 139–40. Actually Richardson was on home leave from roughly the beginning of May to early June. Spence Richardson, telephone interview by the editor, Mar. 13, 2001.

13. Vance had resigned late in April over President Carter's decision, against Vance's recommendation, to use force in an attempt to rescue American hostages at the U.S. Embassy in Teheran.

14. Wickham, *Korea on the Brink*, p. 207.

15. Wickham returned on the nineteenth. For a description of the general's meetings with Korean military officials May 19–24, see ibid., pp. 129–41.

16. Ibid., p. 205.

17. In their memoirs both Ambassador Gleysteen and General Wickham also downplayed the American role in this matter. See Gleysteen, *Massive Entanglement*, pp. 132–33; and Wickham, *On the Brink*, p. 133. For the official U.S. position, see Wickham, *Korea on the Brink*, pp. 206–207.

18. Wickham, *Korea on the Brink*, p. 208.

19. Ibid., p. 207; Gleysteen, *Massive Entanglement*, p. 141.

20. Ibid., pp. 140–41; Wickham, *Korea on the Brink*, p. 209.

21. Wickham, *Korea on the Brink*, p. 209; Gleysteen, *Massive Entanglement*, pp. 142–43.

22. This was done in the document reprinted in Wickham, *Korea on the Brink*, pp. 213–28.

23. Severe gaps remain in the records currently available to scholars. The editor's search of records at the Jimmy Carter Presidential Library confirms the author's conclusion. The documents available in Box 44, Country File, National Security Files, BM, indicate that Donald Gregg was the National Security Council staffer most attentive to the Korean issue during the period and that he followed Gleysteen's suggestions in his advice to Brzezinski.

24. Wickham, *Korea on the Brink*, pp. 209–10.

25. Gleysteen, *Massive Entanglement*, pp. 152–56.

26. For a historian's account of the Iran crisis, see James Bill, *The Eagle and the Lion* (New Haven: Yale University Press, 1988), pp. 292–302. That the Iranian situation influenced the U.S. handling of the Korean case is clear in Donald Gregg's assessment for Brzezinski, May 21, 1980, Box 23, Subject File, DHM.

27. For the editor's analysis of the various pressures facing the Carter administration in May, 1980, and a comparison with the circumstances of 1987, when democratization in South Korea did occur, see Stueck, "Democratization in Korea," pp. 19–24.

28. For a summary of this issue, see Oberdorfer, *Two Koreas*, pp. 133–38. For Gleysteen's coverage, see *Massive Entanglement*, pp. 157–58, 172–76, 188. For Carter administration efforts, see various correspondence, Box 44, Country File, National Security Affairs, BM.

29. Gleysteen, *Massive Entanglement*, pp. 185–89.

30. Wickham left for Washington on May 14, 1980, and did not return until the nineteenth. For his explanation of circumstances, see Wickham, *Korea on the Brink*, p. 125.

Chapter 10. Return to the United States

1. Armitage was appointed to the position of deputy secretary of state in January, 2001.

2. For a useful analysis of the North-South military balance from 1950 to 1990, see Jack E. Thomas, "The Military Situation and Capabilities of North Korea," in *Korean Challenges and American Policy*, ed., Ilpyong J. Kim (New York: Paragon House, 1991), pp. 275–303. For a similar comparative analysis of the economic realm, see Byoung-lo Philo Kim, *Two Koreas in Development* (New Brunswick, N.J.: Transaction, 1992), pp. 65–86.

3. For background on North Korea's atomic bomb project, see Michael J. Mazarr, *North Korea and the Bomb* (New York: St. Martin's, 1995).

4. The first Korean officer in this position was Maj. Gen. Hwang Won Taek.

5. In 1994 the North linked Team Spirit's cancellation to progress on the nuclear inspection issue. Although there was no formal agreement on the matter, the exercise was not held in future years. (See chap. 13, note 3.)

Chapter 11. My Fourth Tour in Korea Begins

1. The activities of 12/12 played some role in the Department of Defense's desire to upgrade the Defense Attaché Office. In addition, by 1987 Korea was more important than had been the case in 1972.

2. In 1996 Kartman was assigned as the deputy ambassador in South Korea and two years later was appointed special envoy for the Korean peace talks with the rank of ambassador.

3. The United States did not establish formal diplomatic relations with the People's Republic of China until 1979. Bush was the head of the American mission in Beijing, in effect, the ambassador.

4. For a solid narrative of events, see Oberdorfer, *Two Koreas*, pp. 162–78. For more analytical accounts comparing the events of 1980 to those of 1987, see Stueck, "Democratization in Korea"; and Fowler, "United States and South Korean Democratization." For an account placed in the context of the political history of the ROK, see John Kie-chiang Oh, *Korean Politics: The Quest for Democratization and Economic Development* (Ithaca, N.Y.: Cornell University Press, 1999), pp. 91–102.

5. Walker's memoirs were serialized in the *Korea Times* during 1997–98. For the section on Walker's approach to the human rights and democratization issues, see *Korea Times*, Aug. 1, 1997, p. W1.

6. By this time the army was firmly in the hands of Roh Tae Woo supporters, but there was little sentiment for direct military intervention in the election. Instead, the military concentrated hard on appearing apolitical, although there were reports that the Defense Security Command would be actively ensuring that there would be a very heavily pro-Roh vote in the military absentee ballots.

7. For reporting on this issue, including its connection to anti-Americanism in South Korea, see *WP*, Dec. 27, 29, 1987, Jan. 9, Feb. 25, 1988; *Los Angeles Times*, Dec. 25, 28, 1987; and *Newsday*, Jan. 31, 1988.

8. For a discussion of issues surrounding the Olympics and the international context, see Oberdorfer, *Two Koreas*, pp. 179–96, 200–201.

9. For news stories on this incident, see *NYT*, Dec. 1, 1987, sec. 1, p. 3; Jan. 16, 1988, sec. 1, p. 2.

10. For coverage of the boxing and other incidents, see James F. Larson and Heung-Soo Park, *Global Television and the Politics of the Seoul Olympics* (Boulder, Colo.: Westview, 1993), pp. 215–27.

11. For press reporting on this incident, see *NYT*, Nov. 17, 1986, sec. 1, p. 14; Nov. 18, 1986, sec. 1, p. 1; Nov. 19, 1986, sec. 1, p. 1; Nov. 20, 1986, sec. 1, p. 8.

12. For news reports at various stages of this incident, see *WP*, Nov. 12, 1986, A23; Sept. 20, 1987, p. C1; and *Times* (London), Apr. 12, 1988, p. 9.

Chapter 12. Duty with Ambassador Gregg

1. See *NYT*, June 20, 1989, sec. 1, p. 22; Sept. 12, 1989, sec. 1, p. 54.
2. See, for example, *NYT*, May 28, 1989, p. 8.
3. On the KCIA, see Clifford, *Troubled Tiger*, pp. 80–86.
4. For good background on this issue, see Oh, *Korean Politics*, pp. 84–89. For contemporary press reports, see *NYT*, Feb. 28, 1989, sec. 1, p. 12; May 26, 1989, sec. 1, p. 4; May 28, 1989, sec. 1, p. 8; July 13, 1989, sec. 1, p. 20.
5. See *NYT*, Oct. 13, 1989, p. 12; Oct. 14, 1989, sec. 1, p. 20.
6. In 1986–87, U.S. exports to the ROK were less than half the value of South Korean exports to the United States. By 1989 the ratio had shifted, but the United States still had a $4.73 billion deficit with the ROK. See U.S. Department of the Army, *South Korea: A Country Study* (Washington, D.C.: Government Printing Office, 1992), p. 337. For a contemporary analysis of the trade issue, see Paul W. Kuznets, "Trade, Policy, and Korea–United States Relations," *Journal of Northeast Asian Studies* 13 (winter 1989): 24–42.
7. *Financial Times* (London), July 19, 1988, p. 1: 4; *Los Angeles Times*, July 24, 1988, p. 1: 8; *Journal of Commerce*, Mar. 3, 1989, p. 5A; Nov. 3, 1989, p. 4B; *Christian Science Monitor*, Mar. 5, 1990, p. 9.
8. Oberdorfer, *Two Koreas*, pp. 186–212.
9. For coverage of the Washington meetings, see *NYT*, July 13, 1989, sec. 1, p. 20; *St. Louis Post-Dispatch*, July 20, 1989, p. 6B; and *WP*, July 20, 1989, p. F3.
10. For samples of coverage of the meetings in American newspapers, see *Los Angeles Times*, Feb. 16, 1990, p. A1; and *St. Louis Post-Dispatch*, Feb. 16, 1990, p. 14A.
11. For press reports at various stages of this controversy, see *NYT*, Nov. 4, 1989, sec. 1, p. 34; *Asian Wall Street Journal*, Jan. 1, 1990, p. 18; Nov. 5, 1990, p. 20; Dec. 10, 1990, p. 3; and *Aviation Weekly and Space Technology*, May 28, 1990, p. 26.

Chapter 13. Journey to North Korea

1. Within two years this observation was officially acknowledged by the North Korean government; shortly thereafter they began to accept, and then to request, international food relief.
2. Much of the dialogue in the meeting with Kim Kwan Jin is from the author's notes and memory. For another source, see the published report *Security on the Korean Peninsula* (Washington, D.C.: International Security Council, 1991).
3. Team Spirit was cancelled in 1992 largely for budgetary considerations, resumed in 1993, but not held thereafter.
4. The following account of the conference proceeding is based on both memory and formal notes. Formal notes were taken by our appointed note taker, journalist Sol Sanders. Additionally, several of the attendees kept field notes. All of these were compared each evening and together formed the basis of a draft document, which our interpreter reviewed. General Stilwell and I then edited the draft report on the lengthy return flight, which was routed from Pyongyang to Beijing, then to Hong Kong, Seoul, and eventually back to the United States. A further edited version of this report was later published by the International Security Council as *Security on the Korean Peninsula*. The account that follows is likely the most accurate and balanced report of the proceedings on the conference in print to date.

5. This concept of a joint team to retrieve and identify MIAs from the Korean War later became a reality. At the time of publication, Americans and North Koreans are working together on North Korean soil, though not without occasional friction, to find and identify the bodies of missing servicemen from that conflict.
6. For background, see Mazarr, *North Korea and the Bomb*, pp. 35–54.
7. See Oberdorfer, *Two Koreas*, pp. 255–67.

INDEX

materiél issues. *See* weapons/military personnel
"Mayumi" bombing, 126
McCullough, Jim, 133
McDonnell Douglas, 140–41
Menetrey, Louis, 121–22, 139
Meyer, Edward, 47
Military Armistice Commission, 81, 118
military attachés, responsibilities, 50, 51–52, 54, 121–22, 135–37
military coup. *See* 12/12 events
military leadership (ROK Army): after Park's assassination, 59–65, 169; characterized, 52–53, 89, 123–24; 12/12 aftermath, 78–79, 80–82, 86–88, 177*n*1. *See also* 12/12 events
military strength. *See* weapons/military personnel
Miller, David, 101–102
Mun Hyong Tae, 178*n*4
Muskie, Edmund, 103

Nance, James, 144
National Assembly, 74, 99, 100
Navy, U.S., 140–41
New York Times, 175*n*11
Nixon, Richard (and administration), 39, 174*n*2
"Nordpolitik," 135
North Cholla Province, conditions, 5–7
Northeast Asia Desk assignment: nuclear proliferation issue, 15–21; Panmunjom tree-cutting crisis, 21–25; responsibilities, 14–15. *See also* troop-withdrawal issue
North Korean National Assembly, 38, 152
nuclear proliferation issues: Park's regime, 15–21; Pyongyang discussions, 157–60; SNIE publication, 16–17
Nunn, Sam, 48

Oh Hung Muk, 162, 163, 164, 165
Oh Tae Bong, 162–63, 164, 165

Olympic Games, 126–27
Operation Paul Bunyan, 22–25
Ormes, Ashe, 57

Pabo (dog), 6–7
Pakistan, 17
Panmunjom tree-cutting crisis, 21–25
Park Chung Hee: assassination, 57–58; Carter's visit, 29, 54–56; defense production, 15–16; nuclear proliferation issue, 16–21; regime characterized, 12, 25–26, 48; student demonstrations, 56–57; troop-withdrawal issue, 45, 49
Park Keun Hye, 29
P3C competition, 141–42
Peace Dam, 128
Pentagon assignment. *See* Northeast Asia Desk assignment
Platt, Nicholas, 176*n*2, 177*n*4
Political Section: after Park's assassination, 61–62, 63; after 12/12 events, 82; Gleysteen-Chun meeting, 94; Gregg's Kwangju visit, 133; Kwangju events, 105; organization, 50–51; ROK election, 126; student demonstrations, 56–57
Presidential Review Memorandum (PRM-13), 40, 45, 176*n*18
Presidential Review Memorandum (PRM-45), 49, 56
Prillaman, Major General, 69
PRM-13, 40, 45
PRM-45, 49, 56, 176*n*18
promotion party (Young's), 65–66, 68
Pyongyang trip: city conditions, 145–50; conference, 154–60; meetings with leaders, 150–54; purpose/preparations, 143–45

Reagan, Ronald (and administration), 47, 111, 123, 168–69
repatriation issue, 156–57, 182*n*5
reports (Young's): 12/12 events, 72–73; FAS field training, 12–13;

Roh meeting, 96–97; ROK Army
    leadership, 53
retirement decision, 142
reunification discussions, 151, 152–
    53, 154
Rhee Byong Tae, 115
Rho Jae Hyun, 64–65, 71, 74
Rich, Bob, 49
Richardson, Spence, 178–79n12
Rogers, Bernard, 42–43, 44
Roh Tae Woo: arrest/trial, 167;
    Blottie meeting, 97; call for
    elections, 122; meeting with
    Young, 95–97; "Nordpolitik"
    policy, 135; 12/12 aftermath, 77,
    78–79, 80; Young's assessments,
    53, 123–24
Ross, Thomas B., 31

Saar, John, 43
sanctions and 12/12 aftermath, 85
Sanders, Sol, 144, 181n4
scholarship proposal, 153–54
security consultative meeting deci-
    sion, 93
Seoul map, 67
Sigur, Gaston, 123
Singlaub, John, 43–45, 46, 47
Sneider, Richard, 19–20, 22, 24, 166
SNIE, nuclear proliferation, 16–17
social activities, attaché responsi-
    bilities, 135–37
Solomon, Richard, 144
Song Ho Gyong, 145, 156–57
Soraksan, 11
South Korea National Assembly, 35
South Vietnam assignment, 7–8,
    27–28
Special Assistant's Office, organiza-
    tion, 50–51
Special National Intelligence Esti-
    mate (SNIE), 16–18
Special Warfare Command (ROK),
    104
SR-71 spy planes, 22–23
State Department: Chung commu-
    nication proposal, 61–62; Park's
    assassination/aftermath, 58, 60,
    63; security consultative meet-

ing decision, 93; statement
    about DPRK rumors, 98; 12/12
    events/aftermath, 70–71, 80,
    84–86. See also specific ambassa-
    dors
Stein, John, 120–21, 123, 124
Stilwell, Richard L.: Panmunjom
    tree-cutting crisis, 22, 24; post-
    Korea work/death, 166; Reagan
    administration appointment, 47;
    troop-withdrawal issue, 43, 46.
    See also Pyongyang trip
Stratton, Sam, 44, 45
student demonstrations, 56, 92, 94,
    97, 98
subway, Pyongyang, 149–50
Syngman Rhee, 101

Team Spirit exercise, 118, 151,
    180n5, 181n3
Third North Korean Tunnel, 36,
    129–30
tobacco trade, 134–35
trade/economic issues: business
    consultation activities, 161–65;
    defense contracts, 134, 140–42,
    181n6; sanctions option, 85;
    tobacco, 134–35
training programs, 8–13, 114–16,
    119, 168
tree-cutting crisis/aftermath, 21–25
troop-withdrawal issue: Carter-
    Park meetings, 55–56; Carter's
    proposal, 40–41, 45–46; civilian
    opposition, 45, 47–49;
    Eisenhower/Nixon opinions,
    174n2; end of, 56, 176n4; mili-
    tary opposition, 41–45, 174–
    75n7; and 12/12 events, 84–85
12/12 events: bunker activity, 68–
    71; impact on U.S. relationship,
    74–75, 78–79, 84–86; interna-
    tional military attachés, 76–77,
    78; U.S. non-anticipation, 64–
    65, 73–74, 169; Young's outside
    excursion, 71–73
12/12 aftermath: countercoup plot,
    87–88; "gag order," 86–87, 91;
    Gleysteen-Choi meeting, 79–80;

ISBN 1-58544-262-3

90000

9 781585 442621